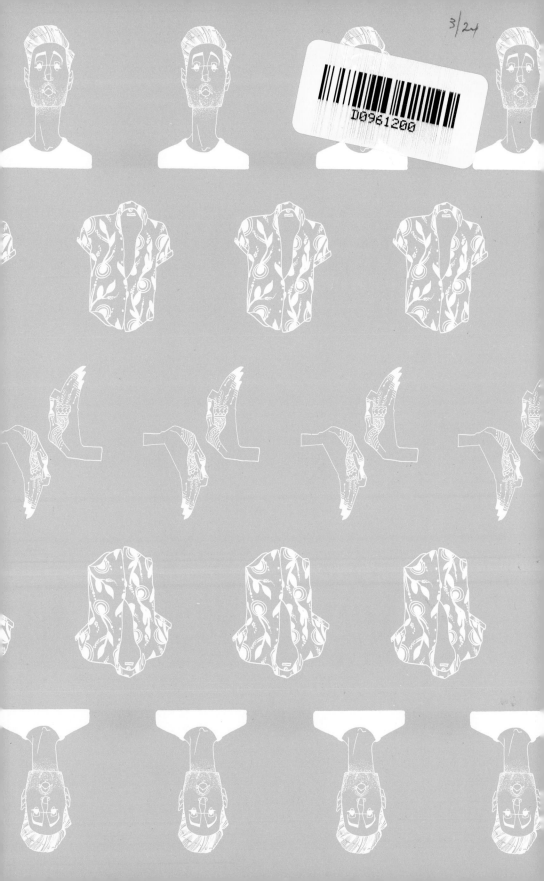

NATURALLY
TAN

TAN FRANCE

M St. Martin's Press

NATURALLY TAN

NATURALLY TAN

TAN FRANCE

WITH CAROLINE DONOFRIO

ST. MARTIN'S PRESS

NEW YORK

NATURALLY TAN. Copyright © 2019 by Tan France. All rights reserved. Printed in the United States of America. For information, address St. Martin's Press, 175 Fifth Avenue, New York, N.Y. 10010.

www.stmartins.com

Designed by Devan Norman

Interior photographs courtesy of the author

Illustrations by Rob France

The Library of Congress Cataloging-in-Publication Data is available upon request.

ISBN 978-1-250-20866-8 (hardcover)
ISBN 978-1-250-20882-8 (ebook)
ISBN 978-1-250-24433-8 (signed edition)

Our books may be purchased in bulk for promotional, educational, or business use. Please contact your local bookseller or the Macmillan Corporate and Premium Sales Department at 1-800-221-7945, extension 5442, or by email at MacmillanSpecialMarkets@macmillan.com.

First Edition: June 2019

10 9 8 7 6 5 4 3 2 1

To my perfect husband, without whom none of this would have been possible. Me and you, forever.

CONTENTS

CONTENTS

CONTENTS

NATURALLY
TAN

SHALWAR KAMEEZ

Straight people love to ask, "When did you know you were gay?" Maybe some people do have an epiphany. I am not that person. For me, when somebody asks me this question, it's the same as someone asking, "When did you know you were a boy?" or "When did you realize you were a human?"

Because I breathe.

I've always known.

It sounds cliché, but I never had that Oprah *aha* moment. I always knew that women weren't for me. Don't get me wrong—I've always loved women, in that I wanted to surround myself with females, and they are the people who have molded who I've become, but there was never a time when I thought a woman was a viable option for my romantic future. I also never thought that a man was not an option. Even when I was very young, I assumed I would get married one day and it would be to a man. Why wouldn't it be so? It was men I was attracted to and loved, so it stood to reason that I would eventually marry one. I never thought that might not be legally possible, nor did I think it was problematic. I was very matter-of-fact about it, as I was with most things in my life, and still am. Throughout this book, you'll realize that maybe I'm not the "zero fucks given" kinda guy, but I'm definitely the "very few fucks given" guy. It's a quality I like about myself and don't plan to change anytime soon.

I grew up in a small English county called South Yorkshire, which is in the north of the country. It was mostly white; there were maybe ten other South Asians in my school and one black student. My parents were both born and raised in Pakistan until they moved to the UK with their respective families in their teens. My dad's family moved to the north of England in the 1950s with very little money. Eventually, he saved enough money to buy a home and start a business, and he became relatively successful. My mum's family was already in a nearby town, and my parents met and—this is very bold of them—had what is a called a "love marriage." In a culture that favours arranged marriages, sometimes even among cousins—(Calm the frack down. I know, I know, that sounds crazy, but I can't get into that right now. More on this later.)—this was an entirely unconventional way to start their life together. We lived in a home adjoining my father's brothers, so I was raised alongside female cousins that I one day might be called upon to marry.

Our home wasn't super religious, but we had a profound cultural connection to our Muslim heritage. Every day, I would get out of school by 3:30, get home at 4:00, and then go to mosque, where I would stay until 7:00. It was like that every day, Monday through Friday, and weekends, too. Even when white school was on vacation, it didn't matter. Brown school doesn't take any time off.

At the age of six or seven, we started to wear modest clothes called shalwar kameez. The pants have an elasticated waistband. If you open them up, they're massive, one size fits all, and they are really bunchy and baggy, tapering toward the bottom with a cuff like a harem pant. Over them, you wear a tunic—for men, plain and over the knees or longer, and for women, looser still. As an added layer of modesty out of the house, women also wear a jilbab—essentially, a large sack. There could be a gust of wind and still you will not see what you should not be seeing.

The only time I was permitted to wear anything other than shalwar kameez was at school, where I wore a uniform, or when we broke out the "fancy Western clothes" permitted for events like weddings or birthday parties.

Beyond this, we were supposed to conduct ourselves with modesty in all aspects of our lives. We weren't allowed to have sleepovers or hang out with our friends outside of school—and we weren't allowed to date. Of course, this was no problem for much of my adolescence, because I didn't like girls. Actually, not being able to date was a blessing at the time, as it made it so easy to cover up the fact that I wasn't into girls. I just couldn't date. *I'm single because I'm not allowed to date and not because I don't fancy girls. So that's that. Nothing to see here, folks.*

There were five of us—I have two sisters and two brothers—and I was the baby. Out of all my siblings, I was always the surest of myself. My parents worked a lot, and so when they weren't around, I watched a lot of TV that was not permitted, like *Melrose Place, Beverly Hills 90210,* and *ER,* all of which had much more mature subject matter than a child should be watching. They dealt with subjects like sex and drug use, which my parents would have been completely shocked to discover I understood, never mind that I was learning about these things from TV. These topics were never discussed in our culture. Because I watched so many shows, I became weirdly worldly wise. My vocabulary was different; I knew things even my oldest siblings didn't know. I was definitely the cockiest one of the family. I would correct other people's spelling and grammar and the way they'd speak. I was the obnoxious sibling. I was a nightmare.

It was clear from an early age that I was "different" and that I had a particular affinity for personal style. Growing up, my favourite movie was *Dirty Dancing,* which no other eight-year-old boy was obsessed with. (Their loss. That movie is still incredible and holds up like no other.) I also had lots of Barbie dolls, but no one outside the house knew about that, which is probably a good thing, as my school was definitely not ready for that in 1990. Weirdly, my dad got them for me. (I know that sounds insane, but here goes.)

My dad and his brother were super close, but strangely competitive. They each had children of similar ages, and the cousin closest to my age was female. She and I were in the same classes throughout school, and we were encouraged to compete with each other when it came to our grades and exams. That competition spilled over into gift giving from our parents.

When my dad learned that my cousin had been given a Barbie house and a Barbie doll, the following week I had a bigger Barbie house with five or six Barbie dolls. I also had two Ken dolls, one black and one white, and a black doll called Cindy who was a popular UK Barbie knock-off. No one saw this as peculiar—which, looking back, just shows how oblivious we all were to Western culture and how that would have been considered out of the norm for most sons to receive. I, however, was over the freaking moon. It felt like all my Christmases had come at once. I wondered when my dad would realize that play-ing with Barbies wasn't what he might have wanted for me, so I always did it in secret. I pretended to be totally unfazed about the Barbies when anyone was around, but as soon as the coast was clear, I'd run up to my bedroom and play house with my new favourite toys. It was a really happy time.

When I wasn't at home, I remember hating school. I found it bor-ing, and I had no desire to learn. I liked the social aspect—I wasn't popular and I didn't have a crew, but I had friends. I had a couple of close male friends, one South Asian and one white, and a really close South Asian female friend. It was pretty easy to make South Asian friends, as there were so few of us that we banded together. Strength-in-numbers kinda shit, because you knew you needed those numbers outside of school, in case it was one of those "special" days when the racist bullies were outside the school grounds waiting for their next attack.

Luckily, I always had someone to sit with or talk to. I felt like I was part of something, and I wasn't concerned about dating or the future. I was fun and funny, and I could make people laugh in class. I think I was liked enough during school hours, and no one at school ever caused me any issues.

Even though I hated academia, I did well in class; I was a solid A/B student. I did no homework, and I did only the minimum required to get through, but it always worked. I remember lording it over my siblings that they had to work so hard for grades (I really was a nightmare with my sibs), and I was able to do it all without revision (our word for *studying*). I didn't have to revise; I could just watch TV instead and then take the exam and do very well.

Outside of school, I didn't have much of a chance to have a social life, as it's not considered appropriate for South Asian boys and girls to mix freely. Even if I had a group of all-male friends, they couldn't come over because I had sisters. At the time, I thought this was so lame, and I was annoyed at my parents for it, but now I see it's just smart, man. As an adult, I now understand they were onto something. I will do the same with my kids. Shit goes down sometimes; you never know! My kids can have sleepovers at our house, where I know that no man is going to do something that he shouldn't. Do you think I'll trust my kids to go stay at some rando's house, with adults I don't know? Heck no.

By the time I was a teenager, I started to panic. I remember watching a movie with my two sisters, featuring a Bollywood star who was very, very handsome. My sister said, "I love him. I want to marry him." I remember saying, "I love him, too. I'm going to marry him, too." And they said, "No, no, boys don't marry boys; boys marry girls."

For the first time ever, I thought, *Holy shit, is something wrong with me? Why can't a boy marry another boy? And why do I want to marry a boy so badly?*

They weren't being mean; that was just what it was like back in the day. I was eight and they were teenagers, and that was the first time someone vocalized it for me. That was the first time I ever thought, *Oh, shit, I'm different, and the thing I thought was okay is not okay as far as other people are concerned.*

As a teenager, I remember having crushes on a couple of people in particular at school. The first time I ever actually realized that I was gay—and by that, I mean I actually associated the word with the feeling—was when I was around thirteen years old, at recess. A friend of mine was playing basketball in the schoolyard. It was a really warm day, so he took his shirt off. I remember looking at him and his muscular physique and thinking he was the sexiest man in the world. That was literally the word I remember thinking at the time . . . about a thirteen-year-old "muscular" guy. Oh my.

I never thought, *I need to put a stop to this.* The only thought I had was, *I hope I can continue to live this way, but I'm going to have to hide it as much as possible.* I came up with a plan I thought would work: I would marry a woman who was my friend, and we would have an agreement. She could date whomever she wanted to date, and I could date whomever I wanted to date. She would be happy, and I would be happy. I really thought this would work.

I was clearly not as smart as I thought I was.

In my early twenties, I thought, *I'm going to have to find a way to come clean.* I knew I was getting to the age where "good" Pakistani boys start to settle down and get married. I could probably make it to thirty at the very latest before people really started to question why I hadn't found a girl and gotten married yet.

I truly never felt wrong about my feelings for men. That's why I still wholeheartedly know there is no nurture involved in any of this. It was all nature; it was all the way it had to be, because it never seemed wrong. I never felt like this was something I had willed, nor was it something I had any control over. It was as simple as lust and love, both of which were completely natural to me.

I did think that when I finally started to date a boy, that's when I would realize there was something really wrong and that I was doing something that was against my community, my culture, my religion . . . everything. I thought I would have a moment where I would feel like I was committing a massive sin.

I have yet to feel that.

Because I grew up in a South Asian community, where you are often reminded you're acting or behaving in a way that would either appease or displease God with everything you do, I expected to feel like I was going against everything my faith stood for. But thankfully, as I grew older, I started to change my mentality. I expected that the first time I kissed another man, I would feel this instant pang of guilt or nausea that would indicate that it was all wrong and that I should stop immediately, but that moment never came. I couldn't imagine that me loving somebody could trigger such an adverse reaction from God. None of us knew, of course. But I truly felt like I wouldn't be punished for loving somebody unconditionally. What could be wrong with that?

But as a kid, this was a tough thing to wrap my head around. This is the case for many gay kids, especially if they're raised within a certain culture of faith. The ideas of heaven and hell were ingrained in my upbringing, as they are for most people in my community. "If you do this, you'll go to hell, but if you do this, you'll give yourself the best shot of not going to hell." It's very much fear-based, and I'm glad that I was able to see that loving somebody didn't mean hell was my only option. I'm sure there were many *other* things I was doing that could have damned me to hell when I was younger, though. Should I go into those? Yeah, probably not. I'm trying to keep up the "good boy" act, and I don't want to ruin that so soon in this book. Read on. I'm sure I'll fuck up that notion for you soon enough.

When I was in school, I always tried so desperately not to cross my legs, even though my legs were begging to be crossed. If I'm really honest, they wanted to do a double cross, which, as we all know, would be such a clear indication that I was into other boys.

I remember very, very early on, I crossed my legs that way once, and a family member said, "Hey, Tan, don't sit like that. Girls sit like that." I couldn't have been older than six or seven, but I was like, *Oh, shit. Why am I doing that if only girls do that? Is something wrong with me?* I tried to train myself to cross my legs the way men cross their legs. I struggled with that almost as much as I struggled pretending to give a shit about watching football on TV, when I clearly just wanted to watch reruns of *Golden Girls* and hang on the lanai, eating cheesecake with those broads. I remember thinking, *But it's more comfortable for me to cross the other way. Who cares if girls are doing it and boys aren't?*

Over the years, I learned to hide away any trait that might give away my sexuality, because I was too busy trying not to make my ethnicity such a big issue. I didn't need a fucking double whammy in my life.

I was too busy being brown to be bothered about who I'd eventually end up wanting to marry. I experienced a lot of racism as a kid, not necessarily at school but with people who lived in my town. I spent so much time trying not to get attacked for being brown; there wasn't a lot of headspace to focus on not seeming gay.

We would get called *Paki* a lot, which is like our version of the N-word. It's a horrible slur for Pakistanis and really painful to hear. Simply getting from home to school and back was very difficult. There were these horrible people in my hometown who would cause us absolute hell. Some were my own age, and some were older. They traveled in a pack, and if ever they saw my siblings or me, they would chase us and throw things and call us Pakis. As a group, we had safety in numbers, but they would try to get us on our own. If you were walking along by yourself one day and you came across them, it was going to be a really shitty time for you.

I had a couple of Pakistani-British friends who I walked to school with. Every now and then, the local bullies would push us around and taunt us. Nothing violent, but a light shoving around to get us geared up for the day ahead. Thankfully, they never beat me up, but they did push me around and take my possessions, and it was still a horrible thing to go through.

Because of this, my family wasn't comfortable with us going outside the house except during school hours. Understandably, my parents were too scared of the racism we suffered in our town. Across the road from our house, there was a little convenience store, which, in England, we call a *corner shop*. We couldn't even go there on our own, because the shop sold cans of beer, and the bullies liked to hang around and drink their beers outside of it.

I distinctly remember if I needed to run across the street to get something, I would go as quickly as possible while my parents watched from the window. How horrifying to think they had to watch their child cross the street just to make sure he wasn't going to get beaten up for being brown. At the time, we were so matter-of-fact about it, and it didn't faze me. Looking back, it was fucked up, and I never want any family to go through that again.

I was a really short kid, usually the smallest in my class and in any group setting. It took me ages to grow. Beyond this, I was a really skinny kid, which made me an easy target. But I was good at running really fucking fast—my hundred-meter sprint was bananas. Racism sucked, but it encouraged me to run faster than the bullies. This is the only silver lining you'll find in this chapter.

One day, I was walking home from school with my brother who's the closest to me in age, just two years older. He was around thirteen years old at the time, and taller than I was, around five foot five. He was a little portly, with super curly short hair. We were near the house, probably only two minutes away, when we saw this group of bullies coming toward us. There were around six or seven of them, about sixteen to eighteen years old, and all much taller than we were. They were all white, sporting unkempt clothes and even more unkempt teeth. They were from the rough part of town, and all of them were familiar to us. They were known in the town for being real hell-raisers and were often in trouble with the law.

To get back home from school, we had to walk on this one road, and there was no getting around them. We looked at each other. *Do we go home? Do we run back to school?* We walked back to school. We waited. We walked back. They were still there. It had been over an hour.

We had to get home somehow. Finally, we were like, "We'll have to go through and pray they don't attack us." We literally prayed. When I was a kid, I wholeheartedly believed you could pray your way out of a bad situation. Maybe this was the moment I accepted the fact that this was not in fact true.

We knew there was no way on God's earth they would ever let us get by. It was the most horrible feeling, walking up to them, the whole time thinking, *Fuck, fuck, fuck, fuck, fuck.* I felt physically sick, my legs starting to turn to jelly. I put on the front of a strong, determined kid, but inside, I was just thinking, *Tan, don't you dare shit your pants. These are the only school pants you like right now.*

When you're a kid, and you see people who are eighteen years old, you see them as adults. These were sixteen- to eighteen-year-old boy-men, and my brother and I were probably eleven and thirteen at the time. There were at least six of them, versus the two of us on our own. I'm no bookie, but gurl, these were not great odds for us, and some real-real was about to go down.

As we got closer, my brother, bless him, was like, "You run. I'll deal with it." We knew there was no way we'd be able to beat them up ourselves, so the only way to solve it was for me to run home as quickly as possible and get help. In hindsight, I wish I had just stayed with him and tried my best to fight them off, or at least encouraged him to run and for me to stay. But he was nowhere near as fast as I was, and in my culture, the older siblings must always protect their younger siblings.

We were only about fifty meters away from our house, which was just around the corner. As we drew closer to the gang of fuckwits, I sprinted around them, into oncoming traffic, ducking and weaving, and lost them. I was home in a heartbeat and ran through the door screaming, "Help! Help! They're going to kill him!"

The look on my dad's face. I had never seen that look before and never did again until the day he passed. It was a look of absolute horror and rage. He knew without me saying another word what was happening. His greatest fear was being realized. As a hopefully soon-to-be parent, I pray I never have to experience this kind of terror.

My dad got up and started running toward the street. Pakistanis usually don't wear shoes in the home, so he ran right out into the street barefoot. Mind you, in England, it's usually cold and rainy and wet, but he ran out there without any selfish concern, as any parent would. I wanted to go, too, but my mum stopped me. Apparently, my dad ran up to the pack of boys, yelling, and they fled. My dad saved my brother, but not before my brother had taken a severe beating. All because we were brown and we needed to get home.

When I was a kid, my fantasy was to one day be old enough and strong enough to hire a van, round up all the bullies in the van, and give every brown person a turn beating the shit out of them. My greatest dream, as a kid, was so violent. I'm not a violent person, and the fact that I would ever dream of this is a good indicator of how rough it was being a person of colour. My biggest fantasy was to be able to take my revenge, which is a seriously screwed-up mentality for a child to have. I once shared this with a friend who is also brown, and he was like, "That's literally my dream, too! To round them up and have them experience what they've done to us."

I had another dream as a kid, which angers me now. But I've talked to many friends of colour who have told me they shared the same dream, and that is to wake up white. I first had that dream when I was very, very young, because I worried constantly that if I went outside the house, bad things would happen to me. It's something I knew I couldn't do anything about, but it did keep me up at night. I didn't tell anyone at the time, as I didn't want to appear weak. Also, none of my siblings seemed concerned that we were different from anyone else, so I thought it best to just bottle it up. I remember sometimes getting anxious when I knew I'd have to walk to school alone, like if my brother was sick. In those instances, I would practically run to school, all the while looking around to make sure that no one was going to attack me for my brown-ness before I got to my destination. I would avoid alleys and often tried to stay close to women or families and pretend I was with them. All the while, I would think, *Why the heck was I born this way?* If I had been born white, life would have been so much easier. I fantasized all the time about what it would feel like to be a white person—nobody would ever comment about your race and how much that must impact your confidence and mood and attitude.

The only nice balancing point was that, in school, nobody ever caused us any issues. I remember incidents of down-low racism, where something would happen and a classmate would say, "Fucking Paki," and then turn to me and say, "Not you. We like you. But *other* Pakis are the worst." And at the time, I accepted it, because I thought, *At least they're not calling* me *that!* Now, I wish I could go back and tell teenage Tan to stand up to their stupidity and ignorance and challenge them. To show them how ridiculous of a statement that was—that because they know me, I'm okay. If only they took the time to get to know others like me, to see just how not-different we all were.

But unless somebody pointed out aloud that I was brown, I often forgot. If somebody called me a Paki, I was like, *Oh yeah! I forgot. I let my guard down for a sec and totally forgot that I should be more aware of it.* I remember very distinctly forgetting a lot of the time, until somebody would very rudely remind me that I was indeed different and how that was not okay.

I remember thinking I always had to be polite, always be nice, always be kind. You can't be another crazy brown person who's upset; you have to show them you're just like they are—bright, white, and smiley.

Now I can process it differently, and looking back, I do feel annoyed at that injustice, because sometimes, no matter who you are, you really do just want to shout and scream about how crappy it is to be treated as less-than. But people of colour are frightfully aware that one person's actions represent the actions of all of our community. A white person can shout and kick and scream, and people will say, "Gosh darn it, this is why we don't like Jack," but they aren't going to say, "This is why we don't like white people." On the other hand, if I did that exact same thing, it would be, "This is why we don't like brown people. Brown people are always so temperamental. They really should go back to their *own* country."

Speaking of that—bitch, this *is* my country. I was born and raised in England. Great Britain colonized my family's homeland, and then that led my people to have the right to come to the UK to settle and have kids in that country. If the Brits could come to South Asia (and many, many other lands) to claim it as their own, then by gosh, I have the right to call England my home, and I will not get out because I'm told to . . . and neither will the rest of my people.

I used to think a lot about how I would react to somebody if they ever tried to fight me. I knew even then that my trying to fight those people was going to achieve nothing, just as my swearing at them was going to achieve nothing. The only way I could make it easier might be to level with them as human beings and try to explain it to them. "You think I'm the devil because I'm brown, but actually, I'm just like you. Yes, my skin and my food might look different, but if you got to know me, you'd probably really like me." Then I would ask them, "Why are you doing this? There's no reason for you to have this hatred for me; it's unfounded. Let's talk about how you came to the conclusion that I don't belong here. And tell me how, exactly, white is right?"

When I was younger, I distinctly remember feeling quite alone. My family wasn't the kind of family that talked about feelings. Well, we told each other if we were mad, but not if we felt something more complex. It's not really the South Asian way to talk about feelings, so it didn't even dawn on me that I should chat to my family or friends about feeling lonely because I never saw our people represented in the media.

I didn't see myself reflected anywhere in popular culture, and a lot of us get our feelings of normalcy or approval or validation from what we see around us. Everywhere you look, you see a lot of Caucasians, and you think, *It's great to be white.* On TV, in magazines, on billboards. It's mostly white. You see black people and you think, *Okay, the tides are turning.* You see lesbians and you think, *Good, we're shedding light on this.* But I do distinctly remember thinking, *Holy shit! I don't see anybody from South Asia on TV who's gay,* and that really started to freak me out.

I thought if I ever came out—because for many years I thought I could hide it forever—it would be a shock to everyone around me because it wasn't something they had seen before.

There was a western British show called *Queer as Folk*, which came out in 1999, around the same time as *Will & Grace* and the original *Queer Eye*. I remember thinking, *Okay, I'm not alone. There are gay people on TV.* But there was a distinct demographic that was missing. I longed for the day when I'd see a bunch of gay South Asian and Middle Eastern men and women on TV and in movies, but it never came. Where were their stories? Where were *our* stories? Had we been forgotten? Did no one want to hear what we had to say?

It took a very long time for this to change. It's shocking that in 2018 I'm one of the first people to do it, but I'm glad things are finally starting to evolve.

When I first considered being on the show, the very idea of representing a community scared the shit out of me, and that was just the LGBT+ community—adding on the responsibility of representing the South Asian community caused me even greater fear. I worried that everything I did and said would be seen as my speaking for the entire South Asian community. That if I said something wrong, people would think even more negatively about Pakistanis than they already might. That if I did something wrong, people would assume all Pakistanis must do this or think this.

I'm hyperaware of the fact that when I speak, I don't speak for just me. The press reminds me that everything I say becomes either the voice of the gay community or the voice of South Asian / Middle Eastern men.

Beyond this, I was so worried about how I was going to tackle religion. I knew that no matter what, I was never going to be just Tan France. The press was always going to refer to me as Tan France, the gay British Muslim. They never introduce Antoni as the gay Polish Christian. Never. He's just Antoni.

Religion was something I never wanted to talk about and still don't. That's my gosh damn business, but the press insists on referring to it in almost every interview or announcement. I was right to worry, as it was something we had to push for every interviewer not to ask about, since it was usually one of the first things they wanted to discuss. I'm more than happy to represent South Asians, but when it comes to religion, that's too personal of a path. I never want to claim to represent a religion or its practices.

So I was so worried to be one of the first, as I knew it would be a hard pill for many to swallow. I knew that I would come up against major opposition from people who wanted to silence me and to pretend that we don't have this issue in our communities. That what I'm doing is "promoting and encouraging" this lifestyle.

No! What I'm doing is a job that I love. A job that makes me happy and that just so happens to offer a perspective that's never really been shown before. No statements are being made. There is no political or cultural agenda. There is just me, being visible and unapologetically authentic.

I hope it provides comfort to kids who have never seen any version of me on TV before. I hope they think, *Tan managed to make things work, and he's happy and open about who he is. I can be, too.*

I hope I give them some hope.

JEANS

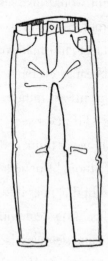

Ever since I was a little boy, I've lived in jeans. Although shalwar kameez was our wardrobe expectation at home, I had a bunch of Western clothing to wear for school, and I would naughtily change into it every opportunity I got. In my adult life, I enjoy denim just fine, but I *loved* it as a kid, because I saw it as playful and experimental.

I'll admit I had a closer affinity than most to jeans, because my granddad owned a denim factory farther up north in England. As a child, I visited him there every summer, and I found it fascinating. The factory was very large, four or five floors, and filled with hundreds of machines laid out in rows. During those visits, I could explore a version of my life that wasn't possible anywhere else.

My granddad showed me everything, starting with the table that held a massive bolt of denim fabric that was then rolled out and cut to size. That piece would be passed on to the next station, where someone sewed a seam. Then on to the next person, who would sew another seam. Each garment would take about ten minutes to make. The reasoning for this process is that if you had one person making an entire garment from start to finish, it would take three or four days, but through piecework, because everyone is so efficient at their one specific task, it takes ten or fifteen minutes. I found the women who worked there fascinating—I'd never seen anything like it. You wear clothes your whole life and never think about how they are produced. But I had this intel that I thought nobody else had, the privilege to see all the work and thought that goes into the things we wear.

My granddad had a licensing deal with Disney, and his factory-made jeans, denim jackets, and sleeveless jackets were printed with Disney characters. I remember thinking, *What? I can make my own Disney clothes?* I wanted to be just like these women one day, screening Mickey onto T-shirts. I saw it as a way to be creative.

As a kid, I wasn't encouraged to be creative. Most children are just told to wear what their parents buy for them—but I was not that child. I saw so many ways to express myself sartorially. I would take as many things as possible from my granddad's factory. I had so many Mickey and Minnie jeans and Pluto jackets. I took every available option in every colour that he'd let me have. I wanted to have as many pieces as possible at my disposal so I could change it up regularly.

I was that kid who changed outfits multiple times a day depending on my mood, all the while knowing that the only thing my mum wanted me to wear was my shalwar kameez.

When I was six, seven, eight years old, I wore multiple looks throughout the day. "It was such hard work to get you to try to stay in the same outfit all day," my mum told me. "You would change depending on what you wanted to do. You would insist on changing for dinner, and then for our evening hangout; if you were going to be playing, you would insist on changing again." When it came to laundry, it was a nightmare. But I had so many looks in my mind that I wanted to put together, much to my mother's dismay!

For playtime, my look of choice was baggy jeans and T-shirts. For dinner, I dressed up in a button-up, done all the way up, and my school trousers. I don't know if I thought my family would pull a "tricked ya, bitch" and take me to the Ritz for dinner, but that was apparently what I was preparing for.

I had only a finite number of tops and jeans, and I wanted to come up with new and different ways of wearing them. I had an industrial sewing machine, and I used it to change things up. My grandfather had taught me how to sew during my summer visits with him, and back at home, I added a velvet collar to a top without a collar that I knew would benefit from it, and I added darts to pretty much every button-up shirt I had to change the way they fit.

Fashion became my thing, because I couldn't express myself any other way. I wasn't a super outgoing kid. I wasn't loud. I was likable because I was friendly, but I hadn't really developed my own personality yet. So I used clothes to show the world who I was. Clothes were the only way I knew how to articulate myself. I never thought it would be my job one day, or that I would wind up working in this industry.

In our culture and community, expressing oneself through fashion was not considered cool—nor was it seen as something boys do—and I found that very difficult. Whenever I dressed myself, I noticed some snickering behind my back. I remember feeling hurt when I heard snickers and comments from family members.

There was one time when I overheard my cousin asking another cousin why my family let me wear that jacket with Minnie Mouse on it when it was clearly meant for a girl. I had never even considered that I shouldn't wear that. I loved it and wanted to wear it. It was one of the first times I realized that people weren't approving of my differences, and it was jarring. No one would ever tell me that I looked stupid directly to my face, but they would kind of make fun of me, like, "What the heck has Tan got on now?"

I couldn't say to anybody, "Hey, guess what? I really like boys," so my style was my way of saying, "I'm all about being who I want to be."

Once, we were headed to a family wedding. Everyone else was wearing these suits, and I wouldn't have been caught dead in the suit that everyone else was wearing. It was boxy, unflattering, and just all-around blah. Even as a kid, I wanted to stand out and make a style statement. On this occasion, I wanted to wear a sports jersey. It was one of those oversized, perforated Starter jerseys for the Mighty Ducks—I didn't even know what team that was or what state they were from—but I saw someone on MTV wearing something similar and so I wanted to rock it, too. I wore it with high-top sneakers and jeans, because it was cool. Or at least I thought it looked cool. It was actually so inappropriate for a wedding. *That's* what I wore to somebody's wedding.

Because I was constantly so headstrong about what I wanted to wear, my parents learned to back off and let me do my thing. They knew that if they didn't, I would sulk all day and cause a scene. I was always polite and kind, but when it came to getting my own way, I knew how to manipulate the situation. I was the youngest sibling. I very quickly learned how to get what I wanted.

It was definitely not what anyone else was wearing, but I didn't care. Gay Tan was here to stay.

It was by hanging at my granddad's factory from a young age that I realized expressing yourself through fashion was even possible—that you can alter and make things that can serve as an extension of who you are. I truly believe that without that exposure, I never would have turned into who I am today. I needed that window into garment production to realize that I could create my own pieces. When I was fifteen, I got my first job at a store, and thus my first paycheck, and I used every penny to have clothes professionally custom-made for me. It was a time before Google, so I used my resources. I found an ad for a seamstress at a local newspaper and arranged to meet her at a tiny little storefront in the quiet part of the shopping area. Inside, the smell of Grandma's house strongly lingered. Even she was surprised that this young guy wanted his clothes custom-made, but she told me she'd give me a fair price, as she was as in love with the clothes as I was.

I was fifteen and getting my clothes custom-made! That's how much importance I put on what I was wearing.

The first thing I had her make me was a camel-coloured jacket (I got the fabric from the local fabric store), which hit just below my waist. It had a full sleeve and a bold, standing collar. It was detailed with brown leather buttons. Perfectly timeless. I had designed this jacket in my head months prior, and it was just as beautiful in person as I'd hoped it'd be. I loved it. I so wish I still had it, but I must have lost it in one of my many moves.

When I was twelve, my granddad's factory closed down, and in the years that followed, I didn't see him as much. He was a typical older South Asian man from Kashmir, which meant he worked hard to provide for his family and was definitely not much of a talker. But once I started my own business, every time I went to his home, I talked to him about my work. My business really brought me back to him. I could tell he was proud of everything that I achieved, because he out of everyone understood how hard it was. He was so shocked that I ended up in this industry. He knew I loved visiting his factory and creating garments of my own, but he never thought I would turn it into a business.

The rest of my extended family did regular jobs—working in fields like finance, for the local council, in HR—that I didn't relate to on any level. They were respectable, but I had no desire to do any of that. I wanted a life that didn't revolve around a nine-to-five that was the same job day in and day out. I wanted more excitement and, quite honestly, I wanted the potential to be wealthy and retire well, not just work to pay the rent and bills. It felt empowering that I had an example in my grandfather and that I was able to say, "I know you may not agree with this, but Big Dad [our term of endearment for him] did this, and it was something to be proud of."

PSA: JEANS

My husband, Rob, is constantly on the hunt for the perfect pair of jeans. He's been on the hunt for years. I have a body shape that lends itself well to jeans—I'm a standard size thirty, and skinny jeans work well on me. Rob, however, has different proportions. He works out a lot and has created a fantastic set of legs and a butt. Lucky me.

He purchased a new pair of jeans every fortnight for like two years until I finally sat him down and said (barked), "There is no such thing as the perfect jean." You can like the jeans, but they'll never be perfect. I would love to say he listened and accepted that fact. He didn't. He just purchases jeans less frequently now, still hoping that the new one will finally work for both his tiny waist and his thunder thighs.

This is true for everybody. Clothes you buy at a retail store aren't for everyone's body. Jeans can be especially hard to find, so you wind up spending hundreds upon hundreds of dollars for jeans, only to discover they're not working for you. To anyone currently hunting for the perfect pair: *they don't exist.*

But when it comes to jeans, my advice to you is to do it in person. Most things you can buy online, but for jeans, it's better to go try them on and purchase them in real life. That's the only way to make sure it works for you before parting with your cash. Also, take a bunch of options and sizes into that fitting room and get to work. This is not the time to be a lazy shopper. Get your arse into as many jeans as possible. They won't be *perfect*, but they'll be the best you can find, because you'll have done all you can to whittle it down to that pair.

If you are desperately struggling with denim, I think the biggest issue people have is the waist. If you've got hips and a bum, you'll need to size up so it fits those parts, but then it won't fit in the waist.

If this sounds like you, then you can get your jeans altered, but it will cost you. You can reduce the size of the waistband or get darts, which will work to get them to fit you better. Go to a tailor who specializes in denim, and have them reduce the waist and keep everything else the same.

If you want to be that hipster cool dude rocking raw denim, just know you're never going to find that perfect fit, because it takes months or even years to break them in and take on your shape. That won't be fruitful for you.

When it comes to denim, as with anything in life, you have to be willing to compromise.

DOS AND DON'TS FOR WEARING JEANS:

DO

- Go for mid-rise, as it is universally flattering.
- Try high-waisted if you're looking to push your style further.
- Go for a slim or skinny leg, which are the easiest cuts to wear.
- Go for darker washes, especially if you're not confident with your style. Darker shades are easier to pair with other clothing.

DON'T

- Low-rise jeans are the least flattering on most body types. Avoid them.
- Those boot-cut jeans make you look shorter and wider. Throw them out. You can thank me later.
- Super ripped or shredded jeans are a big statement, so wear sparingly.
- When it comes to harem / drop crotch, if you're not confident with that style, these are a *lot* of look.

MOUTHWASH

It's amazing how when you're a kid, somebody can mention something once, and it stays with you forever.

I spent so many of my younger years trying desperately to make other people comfortable. If I were in a predominantly Caucasian setting, I tried not to seem too South Asian. I was hyperaware of smells. I never said, "Ooh, let's go for Indian food," because people made fun of kids like me for smelling like Indian food. We couldn't help it, doucheBs; that was what was cooked in our homes. But I was determined to avoid smelling of Indian food at all costs. (Also, side note for everyone out there thinking, *Tan, you said you were Pakistani. What's with the Indian food?* Pakistan and India were the same country until the late 1940s, so our cuisine is one and the same.)

Even though I was so aware of odors, hygiene was something that didn't naturally occur to me. Once I hit puberty, a female cousin who was much older than I took me aside and told me, very casually and calmly, "You've hit a certain age, and you should probably bathe more and start wearing deodorant." I took it to the extreme. I started showering twice a day, every day, and I still do.

It also never occurred to me that oral smells were a thing.

One day in class, a girl was making noise with a couple of her girlfriends, and the teacher told her to change her seat. "Go sit next to Tan," she said.

The girl mumbled, "Not next to dog breath." She had a mean look on her face as she said it. I sat there working away, but I looked up for a millisecond, long enough to see it.

I will *never* forget it—the way it was said, the exact words, the exact tone. It is one of a couple of things I am governed by today that I can never un-hear.

I thought, *Oh my god! I've got dog breath?* I had never even considered what my breath might smell like. That next day, lord knows, I always had a fucking mint in my mouth. To this day, I use mouthwash a minimum of ten times a day. I always carry mouthwash with me. It's a small bottle that I carry around in my bag that holds enough for a good ten to fifteen rinses. If I can't bring a bag with me, I bring along a spray to see me through until I can get home to my mouthwash. I will never, ever get to a place where somebody can say I've got bad breath.

But emotions aside, that comment legit changed my life, and here is why. For most of my life, I was terrified of the dentist. I went as a kid, but I became so afraid that I didn't go back for seventeen years. During that fateful visit, I had a tooth removed, and to do that, they had to inject the roof of my mouth. They didn't use any nitro, so I felt every second of that intense pain. I was scared off for years. When I finally did go (just last year), I only had a couple of cavities. Because I used mouthwash so often, I had miraculously warded off any serious issues. So yes, "dog breath" was one of the worst things anyone could have said to me, but it also fucking saved me.

That girl was the queen bee, but she peaked in high school. Go ahead, have that moment, Emma. She recently reached out to me on Facebook, telling me how she was so proud of how far I've come. I did not respond.

That, dear reader, is the sweetest fucking revenge.

BOLLYWOOD

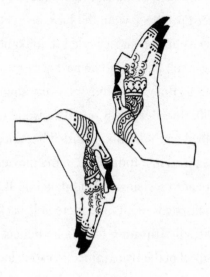

When I was a child, I was *obsessed* with Bollywood movies. Everyone from my community was obsessed with them, too. It's often surprising to Western people, because Hollywood is so massive, but Bollywood is actually bigger. They put out more movies than any other country in the world.

I came to understand the world through Indian movies. The thing I've always found fascinating (and still do) about Bollywood is that it provides a weird loophole in our culture. Growing up, we weren't al-lowed to watch shows or movies that encouraged romantic love—what we called "love marriages." (Now that I'm free from the bondage of my community, I see what a difference this is! As a kid, such marriages seemed taboo and like something only Caucasian people did.)

But in Bollywood movies, the characters were allowed to have love marriages. And because they were brown people who spoke our language, it was okay to watch them. (If these exact same movies had featured white Western people, it wouldn't have been allowed.) I bought these movies to get a glimpse into a world I didn't quite understand—a world I knew we weren't allowed to be part of but wanted to be.

When it comes to Bollywood movies, every single one is a musical. Back in the '90s, there was only one Bollywood movie that wasn't a musical. It bombed and it bombed hard. They tried something different, and they realized that Indians go to the movies very, very regularly and they expect to see singing and dancing. Bollywood movies are always full of saturated colours and incredible backdrops that make the experience visually stunning for the audience. They definitely don't cheap out—most of them are filmed in exotic locations (beaches, mountains, palaces) that transport you to the most magical moments imaginable. It was such a fairy-tale experience for young me, and I wanted to be immersed in it.

More than anything, I wanted to be one of those people in those Bollywood movies. I think even as a kid I knew that I wouldn't be the Bollywood actor who was trying to get the woman. Instead, I thought I would be the one to be saved by the Bollywood actor. And for whatever reason, it never occurred to me that that wasn't an okay belief.

I told everybody who would listen that I wanted to be a Bollywood actor. Now, in order to be a Bollywood actor, you need to be able to act and dance, which I could not do. And here's the kicker—you also need to be able to read Hindi, and I couldn't do that, either. Reading Hindi was the only way you could ever practice and memorize your lines. Yet somehow I convinced myself that I would be such a formidable actor that they would make an exception for me and find a way to help me learn my lines phonetically. Did I mention that I was also completely delusional as a kid?

I remember my siblings taking the piss out of me, saying, "You know this is never going to happen, right, you idiot?"

To which I would reply, "Shut up, man. I'm totally going to find a way to make it happen!"

I was so deluded that when I was a teenager, I decided that when I went to sixth form (a two-year elective program that happens after high school but before university), I would take a performing arts class. Apparently, I thought our sixth-form performing-arts department was so killer that I could learn a new language and become an international superstar within a few short semesters. I clearly didn't realize that it wasn't just one step and then overnight I'd suddenly become the next Shah Rukh Khan (a.k.a. the Indian Tom Hanks).

In the last few months of high school, every student had to go to career counseling to talk about their plans for the future. The counselor was a sinewy woman who looked like she really needed a good meal. She had long brown hair that hadn't seen a brush in a long time, and she had one those faces where, even if she were in the US, you would see her and immediately think, *You've got some strong British heritage going on there, lady.* At the time, I thought she was forty-five or fifty, but looking back on it, she was probably around thirty.

So I told my counselor I was going to be a Bollywood actor. I was

sixteen—and I probably should have known better. But I very confi-
dently told her, "I'm going to sixth form for performing arts, and then
I'm going to move to India to be the next Bollywood star."

She squinted at me, very confused, and said, "Do you really mean
this?" I told her I did. And then she tried to tell me how to make my
dreams a reality. God bless that woman for not laughing in my dumb-
arse face and telling me to plan a backup career. Instead, she started
breaking it down for me. She said, "Sign up for performing arts class,
then take this class to learn to read Hindi, then go to India and see if
you even like being there . . ." She didn't discourage me, which was
probably a flaw on her part (I'm assuming she was fired shortly after
that), because the next thing you know, I joined the gosh-darn performing arts class.

Here's the thing: performing arts *class* is not the same as performing arts *school*. An actual school sounds amazing—you're doing
theatrical shit all day, you're working on your craft, you're learning,
learning, learning. But here, performing arts was just one of three
areas I was concentrating on, and I took a class for one hour, three or
four days a week.

Beyond that, the entire endeavor was a bit, shall we say, challenging for me.

You see, in performing arts class, you had to sing, dance, and act.

As previously stated, I can neither dance nor act, and I most definitely can't sing.

Still, I thought this was a good idea. What the fuck happened to
me as a kid, I don't know. I'm positive somebody must have thrown
me down the stairs one too many times, making me so stupid that I
couldn't see the absurdity of my grand plans.

I used to sing Céline Dion in my bedroom. In particular, I used to sing both parts of the Céline Dion / Barbra Streisand hit track "Tell Him." It's incredible. I stood in my bedroom and rehearsed. *"Tell him . . . tell him that the sun and moon rise in his eyes . . ."* (Wait, have you heard this song? Do you know what I'm talking about? If not, take a break from this chapter to go find it on Spotify and enjoy the splendor of the song. But then come back to me because you and I are only just getting acquainted.) And I thought, *I can hear myself, and clearly I'm great. How have I not been discovered by Simon Cowell or Usher yet?*

But when it came time to audition for the annual musical, the way it worked was that everyone in the class, all twenty or so students, had to sing all at once, and the teachers came and tapped you on the shoulder to sit down, which meant that you sucked. Sure enough, I was the first person to have their shoulder tapped to say, "Sit the fuck down, you dumb bitch."

I did not get cast in the play. So in protest, I didn't go see it. I heard the guy who got the lead went nowhere in life, so there ya fucking go. JK, JK, JK.

Anyway! Every time we had to sing, I would die a little inside, because I realized I couldn't really hold a note.

I also can't dance, but I hide it well in public. What I mean by this is, when I'm dancing in the mirror—and really, who doesn't dance for themselves in the mirror?—I know that Beyoncé would be impressed. I know she would say, "Tan, I didn't even realize that was you and not one of my backup dancers." Alone, I'm incredible. But when I'm dancing and I see other people, my limbs take on a life of their own and they insist on embarrassing me. "You should not do this publicly," they say. So I stop.

Every time we had to do something dance-y in class, I felt this burning, nauseous feeling. I still get that now when I have to do something I'm not comfortable with. Now I understand it's the same embarrassment I felt when we started filming *Queer Eye*, which stems from the fear that people will think you're an imposter. When it came to dancing, I maybe could have done it. But I didn't have the confidence back then to be able to pull it off.

For the final part of the class, in order to get our credits to pass, we had to write a six-minute monologue and perform it in front of the class. Six minutes is a long time to just sit there and talk. Also, again, I couldn't act, which makes said monologue infinitely more troublesome. You know when you look at someone on TV and with every word they speak, you think, *Ooh, that person's terrible. They can't act.* Well, that's how I act. Every time I had to talk, I'd think, *Ooh, Tan. You fucking suck.*

For my monologue, I wrote a piece about a person who'd fallen in love and was trying to tell their best friend they were in love with them. It was so lame, but every kid goes through this, where they fall in love with someone they're friends with. All throughout the monologue, it seemed like it was a girl I was in love with, and then at the end, I said something along the lines of, "I don't know how I'm ever going to tell him."

Bam! Tricked ya, bitch. I thought I was so smart (insert eye-roll emoji).

I actually got a really good grade—I got a B plus, which was shocking because when it came to the arts, I thought I was a very strong F student, and I prided myself on my consistency. That B plus was very exciting for me. But because I felt so nervous, and because I had given away my secret, I decided not to go back to drama class the following year.

Looking back, it wasn't just the singing, dancing, and acting that were problems. From the moment I arrived at performing arts class, I always felt like I didn't really belong. I was one of the first brown people in my town to do it, as people in my community generally discouraged performing arts. My family at least wanted me to do whatever was going to make me happy—as long as I was willing to balance it out with something academic. When you enroll in sixth form, you have to choose three subjects, so I chose psychology, sociology, and performing arts. As long as I was pursuing something in the medical field, they were happy to entertain my ludicrous fantasy, all the while knowing, for them, psychology was the goal.

Still, when I arrived at the first day of class and saw that there were no other brown people, I thought, *Something is weird here.* The other kids were also wealthy and very cliquey. My town had a few different parts to it—a working-class part of town, where I lived, and a part with much nicer homes—all of which were represented in my high school. The kids in the performing arts class were the fancy kids who had taken ballet and music classes their entire lives. They all knew each other already, and I felt very much excluded. No one was ever mean to me, but they clearly had no interest in being associated with me.

My own very short foray into music was the violin when I was eleven. There was a successful violinist at the time called Vanessa Mae, who I thought was so talented, and I wanted to be able to play the violin like she did. Her take on pop violin really was my weird preteen jam.

It had been so difficult to convince my dad to let me do it. The violin itself was expensive, and we didn't have a lot of disposable income. And the classes themselves cost a lot. More importantly, I'm sure my dad was hyperaware of what a complete lazy shit I was and that there was no way on God's green earth that I would commit to learning a new skill. I swore that I was going to excel at it, and it would be great for university applications.

About two classes in, I thought, *Holy fuck, I've made the biggest mistake. My dad is going to kill me.* I stopped taking the classes, but because I didn't want to deal with the confrontation of telling my family, I continued to pretend I was still going.

My dad passed away very shortly afterward, before he found out I was quitting the violin, so I never got in trouble for it. If I remember correctly, horribly, I used it as a good time to announce to my mother that I was going to quit the violin, so I was able to bury that nugget along with everything else that was going on at that time.

But performing arts class wasn't entirely bad. Even though the majority of the kids were different from me, it was there that I first noticed there was another gay student at our school. He never mentioned it directly to me, but he was rather effeminate and loved a Judy song. He was the first person I got to know who was gay. At least, I think he was gay. Maybe he was just a very effeminate straight guy. No, he made a killer friendship bracelet. His fucking bracelet-making skills were insane, yo. He had to have been gay.

Everyone in class was very loving with him. They were kind and inclusive and laughed at his jokes. And the more flamboyant he was, the more people enjoyed him. He was the first person I encountered where I thought, *Oh, shit, I'm not the only one in school.* I knew there were other gay people out there in the world at large, but in our school,

I hadn't known anyone else. They were all clearly doing what I was doing (even if it was not quite convincing). Playing it straight. I had thought I was very much alone, and it was nice to discover that I wasn't.

He and I never really spoke, as he was one of the kids from the other side of the tracks, but it comforted me to know that I was not alone at school.

Recently, I was going through a pile of old belongings when I stumbled across my record of achievement, which is a folder containing your high school grades and certificates and records of your achievement that you'd present to each potential university or employer after graduation. I hadn't seen it in decades. For part of it, you write a cover letter, and in my letter, the very last sentence is something along the lines of: "I want to study psychology and sociology at university, but my true passion has always been to be in show business. My hope is to be a host or a presenter on TV someday."

I hadn't seen this since I wrote it at seventeen years old. Now I look back and say, "Who the fuck was that? *Who* wrote that?" I don't remember writing it. I don't even remember thinking it. I distinctly remember wanting to be Bollywood's next answer to Tom Hanks, but a host? Still, it's very bizarre that that's where I've ended up. The weird thing is, I didn't mention clothes or fashion design, which I so desperately wanted to get into. I find it strange that I left that out in favour of TV. Bollywood wasn't meant to be, but it appears I always knew I was destined to wind up in entertainment.

NOKIA 6210

By the age of seventeen, it was clear that the performing arts were not my calling.

But I knew that I loved fashion, and I decided to find a way to make that a thing. So after my first year, I dropped out of sixth form and signed up for fashion college in my hometown. I didn't tell anyone what I was up to. I did it for a whole year before I had the courage to tell my family, "Guess what? I'm not going to sixth form anymore! I'm not doing something academic. I'm not going to be a doctor of anything. I'm going to fashion college." I knew that news wouldn't be well received, and I was right. In our culture, the only options are to be a doctor or lawyer. So I didn't ask anyone's permission before moving forward, because I knew they would say, "What can you possibly achieve with this?"

It was the best thing I ever did. Within the first couple of months of attending the college, I'd gotten to know so many people. I had a crew of creative friends who were great. They were a little more flamboyant than other people I'd encountered, and there were loads of gay people at the college. None of them seemed to want to be my friend, but who cared? I had found my place. I loved my courses, and it felt like the right move for me.

Still, I knew if I told my mum, she would try to get me to drop out. To tell my mum I had enrolled in this two-year fashion course was as bad as me saying, "I've gotten a girl pregnant." It was such a big deal.

Sure enough, when I broke the news to my family, they said, "Why are you choosing to do something creative? This is a course for girls! You can't make a living out of this!" Some people are so concerned with their kids pursuing an arts course, like you're just flitting through life if you're doing something creative. Gone are the days where that mentality is even plausible. There are so many great creative roles out there where you can earn a truly good living. There is no reason to think this way.

Back in the day, people saw art college as a risky move. I remember having a conversation with my whole family, sitting them down and saying, "You know me. You know I'm responsible. I don't make decisions lightly. If I say I'm going to turn this into something, you know I'm doing it because I truly believe I can."

I assumed blood would be shed and I'd have to hide my family's bodies in the backyard. Thankfully, that wasn't the case. Although no one took it super well, they did all come around after a couple of days.

That was always my way. I am very good at talking people around. It wasn't manipulative; I was just a really good salesperson, and I could show them why my way was better. I think had I been from a stricter South Asian family, it would have been a problem, but my family was willing to let me see it through. When they saw how much effort I was putting in, they were really accepting.

Still, I had been wise to wait to break the news. If I had told them initially that I was dropping out and starting fashion school, I think they would have had a heart attack. You see, kids, sometimes lying is for the greater good.

A lot happened to me at age seventeen. It was a really good year. I enrolled in fashion school and started something I wanted to do, I had a great-paying job for a seventeen-year-old, I got my first partner, and I traveled to New York for the first time. Fashion school is also where I came out for the first time.

When I came out to my best friend, Kiri Pearson, it was a big moment for me, as it is for anyone. I had been dating a super nice guy from work called Dave. A few weeks into dating Dave, I was desperate to tell my best friend. I wanted to scream it from the rooftops. But I didn't have the balls to tell her to her face. I tried so many times to say the words, but every time I got close, I started to feel like I'd throw up, so I'd bottle it.

This was back in the day of the Nokia 6210, which is a tiny little phone where I could type out a text with one thumb and not even have to look. I would use it under the desk and compose a whole message with no mistakes. I didn't have many skills in life at that time, but I was very proud of that one.

One day we were in class, and I said via text, "I met someone! We're dating."

She replied, "Oh my gosh, what's her name?"

I wrote back, "His name is Dave."

Without skipping a beat, Kiri said, "That's wicked, tell me more about him."

And I felt this incredible sense of calm wash over me. She wasn't treating me any differently. I turned to her, I gave her a hug, and then we gossiped like any friends do when you first start dating someone.

I went home that night on top of the world. I could finally tell other people. I realized I could tell my friends, and they wouldn't hate me, they wouldn't judge me for it, they'd just accept me no matter what.

I'd love to say that I told everyone in my life, and they were all happy and we all lived happily ever after, in our open-minded, loving world. But not all my friends were so great.

I had two other close friends, both of whom I'd known for over ten years. I loved them and assumed they loved me unconditionally. After I started dating Dave, they decided to follow me one day after our friend hang, as I'd been rather evasive about why I'd been less available to get together. I only heard about this after the fact, but apparently, they trailed me home from school and hid across the road to see where I was going and watch whatever was about to happen. When I gave Dave a hug and kiss, they realized. The jig was up.

These two friends were South Asian and were raised in homes with similar ideals to my own. They weren't used to seeing gay people, and they didn't know how to process this news. They stopped talking to me that day, and within days, I heard from a couple of mutual friends how disgusted they were and that they'd started to spread rumours.

Immediately after they followed me, they started to tell people I was dating a guy, and more and more people began to find out.

These girls had been my friends since I was seven years old—which, by age seventeen, was the majority of my life. They knew what their rumours would do to my reputation in my tiny South Asian community. I was heartbroken. I went home and cried. I didn't want to leave the house for days, but when I finally did, I sought comfort in the friends who loved me unconditionally.

They tried to call me a couple of times over this period, but I chose not to answer. I knew their comments would be mean. We'd never talked about gay people before, and I didn't know what their feelings were. But once the rumours started, I knew.

We never spoke again after that time, and I haven't seen them since. I've never so much as run into them on the street. One of them tried to reach out via Facebook a few years ago. She tried to add me as a friend, and I rejected it immediately.

I think the world has changed, and by now they've probably had more exposure to the gay community. When you're seventeen or eighteen, you have opinions about everything, and sometimes those opinions change. But I was so hurt by them at the time that even if they have different views, I have no desire to hear that now. That's for their new friends and family to benefit from; I have no desire.

As more and more people heard the news, I was essentially dragged out of the closet, so I had no choice but to leave town. Thankfully, this all happened toward the very end of my fashion course, while my family and I were making a long-planned move to Manchester, so I was able to escape my small town before the rumors made their way to my home. I wasn't quite ready for *that* conversation. Baby steps.

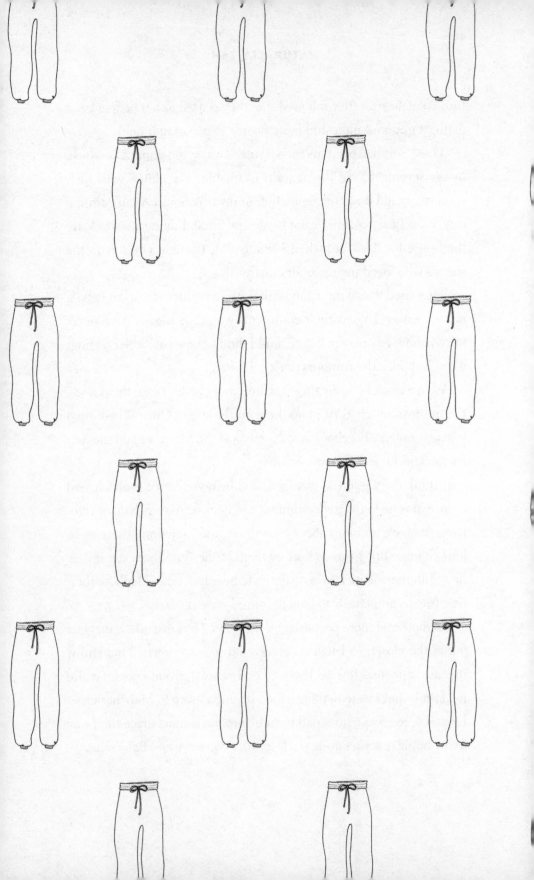

SWEATPANTS

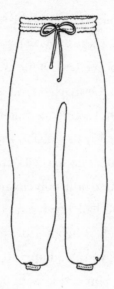

When I was in college, I got an evening job at a call center. I would go to work Monday through Friday, straight after my classes, which is something I wish more students would do. It teaches you structure and responsibility, and it affords you some extra money to spend on new shoes.

I had already been working there for a few months when one day, my friend was driving me to work. As we pulled up to the building, I saw this guy and his friend walking out the main doors. I remember thinking, *Holy shit, who is that? He's beautiful.* He had fake-tan skin and blond hair and was dressed nicely (for that time, because the early 2000s weren't known for great style moments) in a nice-fitting T-shirt and jeans. He was clearly on the daytime shift, as he was just leaving when I arrived. Just as quickly as I saw him, he was gone. But I kept thinking about him. I thought he was the most beautiful guy I'd ever seen in person.

Just from the look of him, I could tell he was gay. There was something about him. Perhaps it was the way he saw me notice him. The first time he saw me, he looked back at me and smiled, and I thought, *Ah, he's gay, and It. Is. On.* Or maybe it was all just wishful thinking? I didn't know, but my gosh, I wanted to find out.

The call center was large, with probably three hundred or four hundred people working there. The lower floor, where we worked, was full of rows and rows of these little cubicles, and the second floor had a balcony where you could look down onto the sea of them. The cubicles came up to about chest height, so when you sat in them, nobody could see you unless you stood up.

I kept thinking about him and how I could find a way to talk to him, but I wasn't going to act on it. For one, I wasn't out to the world yet, and I was too scared of anybody knowing. But I needed to find a way to see him again. A few days later, I went to work early. I planned to hang out in the cafeteria and eat before my work started. But after I got my food, I strolled up and down the aisles, looking around like I was searching for something other than this guy. I was so smart and not completely obvious about it at all.

Then he stood up. And I saw him.

He was wearing his little headset, as he was on a call. We looked at each other and smiled.

For the next month, I would go to work early every few days. I would stroll around looking for nothing in particular until Dave would stand up and smile. (For the record, his name isn't actually Dave, but he was a generic white guy, and Dave sounds pretty generic to me, so there you have it.)

And then I heard some gossip about him from somebody we both knew. They'd said that he was possibly going to have to move to another sales team, as people weren't getting along with him. It wasn't a big deal, but it was the only way I could think to have a conversation with him. So I wrote him a note, saying something along the lines of, "I need to talk to you about something being said about you. If you'd like to get together, here's my mobile number." I was so nervous walking up to his cubicle. As I walked down the row, a few people looked at me like, *What the fuck are you doing in our pod?* Finally, I got to his desk, where I basically dropped the note and ran. I felt like I was going to shart my entire organ structure out of my body right there and then.

He didn't text me for a couple of hours, even though I knew his shift was long over. I started to panic, thinking, *What if he's not gay and knows it was clearly a pickup? What if he told people at work and now everyone will know?*

Finally, I got a message. "Hey, it's Dave. I'm interested to hear what you know."

I wrote back, "I'd rather talk in person."

He immediately responded, "Do you want to come over?"

I was like, *Fuck yeah I do.*

So I went to his apartment. I was so nervous. I was only seventeen. At twenty-two, he was a full-grown man. That felt like a big deal at the time. He lived in a large four-story house with a bunch of friends, including a couple of other gay guys. It was the first time I'd ever hung out with gay men.

He took me straight up to his room, because it was his only personal space in the house. The room was super neat and tidy. That didn't surprise me. He was really well kempt, so I assumed his home would be, too.

I told him the gossip, which wasn't a big deal. We established that he was gay and that I was gay. And then we kept talking. He had a sweet personality but was more direct than I was expecting, and he had a sassy side to him. He didn't work out but was naturally in great shape, and I remember thinking his legs were great. And he had the bluest eyes I'd ever seen. I had to stop myself from staring at them.

I had my first kiss, and it was beautiful. It wasn't anything too much—a slow, long kiss on the lips. The perfect, first, rated-PG kiss. By the end of the visit, it was around two in the morning. I had to go because I had college in the morning, but I told him I liked him and if he wanted to go out sometime, I would love that.

We agreed to meet the next night. We continued to meet every night for the next few weeks, but it started out just at his apartment. Living in such a small town, I didn't want to risk bumping into anyone I might know, so we usually just hung at his place with his friends. Then, a few weeks into our relationship, I started joining him and his friends on nights out to the bars and clubs in neighboring cities. It was all so new to me, and I didn't think I liked it. I knew I had to go if I wanted to keep him in my life, as this was something he and his friends loved, but I only went to be a good partner. Don't get me wrong—I sometimes had a blast. If the music was great (and by great, I mean '90s hip-hop), I would tear up that goshdamn dance floor, but usually we went somewhere that only played club music, and so I would just hang at a table hoping for the night to be over. On the whole, I knew it wasn't the life for me.

After a couple of months, we talked everything over and decided we wanted to be exclusive. And so, after a year or so of dating, we got an apartment together in Manchester, after my family had already moved out there. None of my family members knew about any of it. They assumed I had a housemate.

Even though we lived together, our relationship was very on again, off again. We had a lot of differences, and we argued often—I didn't like how much he drank, and that wasn't going to cut it for someone who was in the gay community. When he drank, he would get a little too sloppy, and I just wasn't into being embarrassed or having to make sure he didn't do anything silly that either of us would regret the next day. In the UK, to be a part of the gay community, everyone would go out until 3:00 a.m. on Friday, Saturday, and sometimes Sunday, and then do it all over again the next weekend. He would drink; we would fight, break up, and then make up, again and again.

He clearly wasn't the partner for me, but he was a great starter boyfriend, and he taught me a lot. I went to my first nightclub with him and had my first drink with him. And through this, I discovered that it was not the life for me. I would join Dave and our friends at the bar for light drinks and chat. Then we'd move on to a club when the bars started to wind down. Then we'd drink and dance until super late into the night. I have nothing against anyone who's into the bars-and-clubs scene; many of my friends frequent them regularly. It's just not my happy place.

After a few years of breaking up and making up, I got the feeling that he was about to break up with me for good. At this point in our relationship, we fought more than ever, and the fights often became really nasty. I would swear at him, and he would swear at me. We were hurtful with each other.

Many times we fought and then slept in the same bed, as far away from each other as physically possible. This was one of the most horrible times of my life. That feeling—where the person you're in a relationship with wants to keep their distance from you, and vice versa—was heartbreaking. It became such a regular occurrence that it was clear to me our time together was drawing to an end. But I knew I would never be the one to leave. He was my first boyfriend, and even though it was clear we were terrible for each other, I was too scared to risk no one ever wanting me again, so I was willing to tough it out.

Thankfully, that was the first and last time I allowed myself to feel that way with a partner—to feel like if it all ended that I would never be loved again. I'm so relieved that it's something I only had to experience once. That shit was crippling.

I had changed so much over the four years we'd been dating. Because I was so unhappy, things like self-care fell by the wayside. I had no desire to get dressed up nicely for him, to make an effort to be desirable to him. These were things that I could have done to try to get that spark back, but I was letting myself go more and more by the day.

Finally, the day arrived. I had been gone the night before, and when I returned home, I found all his bags were packed. I knew full well we had been fighting all the time. I was a different person back then because our dynamic was so unhealthy. Still, I remember seeing his bags and thinking, *What's going on?*

"We're not getting along," he told me. He sat on the sofa. He was calm. Not angry at all. Not mean. Just honest. "You're not the same person you were. You've let yourself go." That's the one real thing I remember, how painful that was to hear. He said I never wanted to go out anymore, that I never wanted to get dressed up.

"You get so dressed up for everybody else," he told me. "But I only get the worst version of Tan. The Tan who makes no effort."

I sat there on the sofa in my terribly unflattering sweatpants. That hit really hard. I didn't know what to say. Then he told me he was done. He said he was leaving, that he didn't want to be in this relationship anymore.

In shock, I walked him to the door, and we said goodbye. Then I came back inside, slid down the wall, and collapsed onto the floor, where I cried for what felt like hours and hours. I thought that only happened on TV.

We had broken up for real, and I went crazy. I'd never had my heart broken before, and I didn't know how it felt to be broken up with. I couldn't believe it had happened. It felt like it would never get better.

At first, I thought, *I haven't let myself go!* But over time, I realized he was absolutely right. I freaking hated when he was right! The only time I made an effort was for other people. The only version of me he saw was the one that made no effort, disheveled Tan at home in his baggy sweatpants and unflattering old T-shirts. That was such an eye-opener for me.

I never made that mistake again.

A lot of us fall into that trap, where you make an effort for everyday people who are insignificant to you. We should make that same amount of effort for our partners, who are the most important people in our lives. They shouldn't be the ones who get the laziest version of us. Yes, we want to be comfortable enough to not have to put on airs and graces for them, but that doesn't mean making no effort to be desirable for them.

On *Queer Eye*, people say they've let themselves go and will share how it's impacted their marriages. But when they start to present themselves differently, that one thing changes so much about their lives and how they view themselves. Do I think you have to be somebody you're not? No. Should you be comfortable around your significant other? Yes, of course. But I think you should make an effort for them, because it's about respect—the respect you have for yourself and the respect you have for your partner.

Do I sometimes sit around the house in my sweats? Yes, sometimes I do. But they are the nicest sweatpants I can find, which complement my physique and are clean. And I'm showered and still presentable. I have nothing against sweatpants if they look good. The problem is more about when you've put no effort in whatsoever. Both you and your partner deserve more than that.

One day, I'll achieve my dream of finally having kids. And then I'll wear sweatpants all the time and write a book about how much I regret having kids, because two-year-olds are a frickin' nightmare and I cannot wait to ship them to boarding school. Then when people ask me, "Tan, why are you in sweatpants?" I can very calmly reply, "Bitch, you try having four children."

In the meantime, though, I will make an effort.

I'm glad Dave was the first person I dated, because he's a really nice person, a good guy who taught me so much. He wasn't the right guy for me, but I still love and care for him very much. We've remained friends over the years. Every few months, we'll message via social media, and we get together every couple of years when I'm back in the UK. And thanks to him, I've learned to never let my partner see me looking unkempt in my ratty ol' sweats.

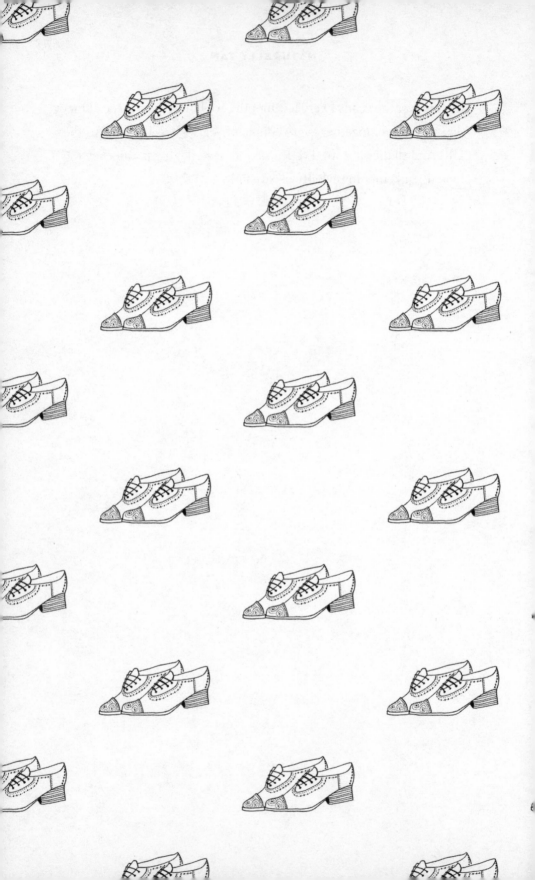

BROGUES

When I was seventeen years old, I had my part-time job at the call center, where I sold phone and internet lines over the telephone. It was not a job I'd dreamed of having, but it paid well, and it was something I knew I could do. All I had to do was talk to people who called in and sell them on something. I'm not really sure how I excelled at it, because I was just a kid, but I was very convincing, and I got a nice commission at the end of every month. Even though I was still living at home at the time, I didn't actually save any money, because I liked to spend it unwisely. To be more exact, I'd spend every penny I made on clothes and shoes.

That same year, I found this pair of brogues (what Americans call *wing tips*) that changed my life. I had seen them at a store, but as was often the case back then, I was out of money. I'd spent it all on other crap I didn't need within the first week of receiving my paycheck. As soon as I had the money again, I ran straight to purchase the brogues, but they were no longer available. I was mortified. I was very dramatic about missing out on sartorial opportunities.

Months later, I was in an outlet store where I discovered they had just one pair of the brogues. As luck would have it, they fit me perfectly. Even more incredibly, instead of costing £150 (which back then was close to $300) they were available for only £20. I was like, "Let's pack them up *now*."

They were a camel/taupe-y colour that looked beautiful with my skin tone. The cut was slightly narrow, which I loved, because it made my feet petite and slender. They had a bit of a lift—just an inch or so—and they made me feel tall. They were technically a special occasion shoe, but they looked great with absolutely everything. I wore them all the time.

At this same time in my life, I started to become an unruly boy. I loved to do things that I knew were wrong. All my South Asian friends and I learned to lie to our parents early on, which was a necessary skill in such a strict community. Up until this point, I hadn't had much of a social life. I had never asked to go outside the house after school hours. I didn't go out on the weekends. I didn't even do things with friends. (This was all pre-Dave.) So when I started to sneak around, they didn't think anything of it. "If he says he's studying, he must be studying!"

In high school, I used to go to the mall on Wednesdays, when I was supposed to be in phys ed. I *hated* phys ed. I had this weird party trick, in which I would kind of pop my arm out of its socket, which I demonstrated for my phys ed teachers so they'd think I was injured, and then I would go shopping. In England, cutting class was called *twagging school*, and if anyone caught me twagging, I would be in so much trouble. So I went to the next town over, to the Meadow Hall Mall, because 1) they had an H&M, and 2) nobody would catch me.

One day, I came up with a stupid idea to go to New York. I had always wanted to go, and somehow, I saw it as completely feasible to make this trip as a seventeen-year-old. Surprisingly, my friends were just as eager to be dumbasses and had zero reservations about going along with my plan.

I told my mum I was going to stay at a friend's house across town and that I would be gone for five days. She thought nothing of it, because I was such a "responsible kid," so it wouldn't have dawned on her to check with my friend's parents to make sure that I was actually going over there to stay.

Instead, I booked a flight to New York City with three of my friends. We booked the flights and hotel through a travel agent we found in town. Mind you, we had never even been to London at that point, but we decided it was perfectly appropriate to go on vacation to a foreign land. It was baptism by fire.

I already knew how to use the train, from my days skipping phys ed on Wednesday afternoons to go to the mall. The train station was only a five-minute walk from my home, and from there, the airport was easy to get to. My friends and I had flown to South Asia enough times to know how the airport worked, so even though we had never travelled on our own, it wasn't a complicated process. Once we were on the American side, we hopped into a taxi and were in the city before we knew it.

Since I had gotten so good at hiding what I was up to, my mum and my siblings, bless them, decided to trust me. They were all like, "Oh, he's Tan. He's the reliable one." They never in a million years expected I had gone someplace else—and that the place was on the other side of the Atlantic.

I knew you had to be twenty-one to get into an American night-club, but wearing my brogues, I managed to blag my way into a night-club with my friends Nasrin, Yasmin, and Bina. All South Asian. All my age. All super cute. And all as willing to lie their way into a club for some much-needed dance release. (Sometimes, with South Asian kids, it's hard to tell how old they are because they can grow facial hair really young. I could grow a full beard by the time I was seventeen!) I even got into Jay-Z's club, 40/40, and I felt really special. I thought I was so mature. It was the first club I'd ever been to, and I thought it was incredible. The music was exactly what I loved at the time—a mix of hip-hop and R&B. I danced until the wee hours of the morning and felt like a freakin' baller.

For five days, when we weren't getting into clubs, all we did was shop, shop, shop. At the time, I wanted to be Missy Elliott with my Timberland boots and hoodies, and in America, Timberlands were half the price compared to UK prices. I bought seven or eight pairs! Every colour I could find. I even kept them in their boxes so they would stay pristine. Between Von Dutch hats and Timberland boots, I was set.

It was, sartorially, a dark time for me. (There is no photographic evidence of this, thank God.) None of us were really photo takers, so we didn't think to buy a camera for the trip. However, there is one hoodie from that trip that I still wear to this day. That was seventeen years ago! So I guess it wasn't all wrong.

I called my mum every couple of days using these ten-dollar phone cards that gave you an hour's worth of call time. I'd seen my mum use them to call people back in Pakistan, so I knew how to place international calls. My first trip went off without a hitch, and so I started to make it a more regular thing, going to New York a couple of times a year.

On that first trip to New York, I made it back safely. However, I am sad to report that my brogues did not. When I unpacked, they weren't in my suitcase. *How could I have lost them?* I called the hotel and accused them of lying. How was it possible no one had found them? They stole them! They saw the beauty of those shoes, as anyone would. "Just send them back to me!" I pleaded. But they swore they were nowhere to be found. They never turned up.

To this day, I'm still sad about it. *Who found you?* I'll wonder. What a treat for that person. If I still had them, I would wear those shoes to this day. That's how perfect they were.

I never told my mum about my travels, because it wasn't a massive issue. I still haven't, though I guess I just did. (Oops, sorry, Mama.) My friends never told their parents about their secret vacations, either. Our parents always told us that we weren't supposed to spend our money on selfish things like clothes or vacations. Our only vacations were meant to go home, to Pakistan. In that climate, lying to our parents was so much easier and made much more sense. Do I think it's right to lie? No. Did I feel it was necessary at the time, to keep the peace and toggle the slack line between my English and South Asian upbringing? Heck yeah.

Now of course, if one of my own children ever did this, somebody would have to die. There is no way on God's earth I would ever let my children go from here to London at seventeen years of age. I look back on my adventures and think, *You moron, nobody knew where you actually were. Anything could have happened to you, and you would have been all alone in a foreign land.* But at the time, I thought I had the mentality of a thirty-five-year-old. We all remember that feeling, I'm sure.

The moral of the story is this: when you love something, always, always buy a second. Hopefully, you will continue to love it for years and years.

Losing those brogues changed the way I shop. If I find a great-fitting pair of jeans, I'll get them in another colour. I have a pair of black boots I love so much that I went and got two more pairs, because they'll never go out of style. If you find a well-made item that is relatively classic and a good foundation piece, *always* buy multiples.

I'm still searching for those brogues. It's been seventeen years, but I continue to Google to try to find something comparable to that pair of shoes. But there was just something about the art of those shoes that cannot be replicated.

It would be incredible if one day my mum tells me that she's had them for all these years. I keep waiting for the day when she's like, "Here's your fucking shoes, you douchebag. I knew you were in New York the whole time."

HAIR

I think it's funny I've become known for my hair.

My hair was never a thing. In fact, until recently, my husband was the one whose hair was always a thing. For the last ten years, anywhere we'd go, people were always stopping him to talk about his hair. He has better hair than I have: it's dirty blond, peppered with grey. He blow-dries it up and out of his face, similar to mine, but his hair has extra height and a slight curl that I can't pull off, as whenever I embrace my natural curl, I start to look very typically South Asian. You South Asians will understand that all too well. When I sport it that way, people begin to assume I'm fresh off the boat. Rob's hair is kind of like an old Hollywood star's hair on their best day. However, since I'm the one who taught him how to style it, yeah, I'm going to take some of the credit. Judge me all you want.

My hair, though, is another story.

I remember thinking, even when I was as young as six or seven, *Gosh, I hate my hair.* I got it cut every two to three months, and I wanted so badly to get a cool haircut. But, like typical South Asian parents who wanted to get the most bang from their buck, my parents had the hairdresser cut it as short as possible.

We went to a salon literally a stone's throw from my house—it was two doors down. It was everything you'd expect from a neighborhood salon. It was pretty, pricey, and everyone wore black. The girl who cut my hair was my go-to from the first haircut to my last at that salon, before I moved at the age of ten. She would give me the "short back and sides, and an inch off the top," which left me with what was close to a crew cut. My features were way too large to accommodate that kind of cut, but looking cute was definitely not the objective for my parents.

I get it—as a parent, you don't want to take your kid for a haircut every two or three weeks—but every time it grew out, I wanted so badly to just get a trim. Just a little bit of something that would make me look less dorky than the cut I had.

It was the '90s, and the other kids, usually the white kids, had a haircut we called *curtains*, where the hair was kept as a long fringe and parted in the middle. It usually had a shaved or shorter portion on the bottom. It looked like something from *90210* or like a very young Leonardo DiCaprio or David Beckham.

This was the first time I realized there were a lot of differences be-tween the white kids and me, besides the colour of my skin. The white kids were able to take pride in their appearance in a way the South Asian kids were not. Attractiveness was not on anyone's agenda in our community. Everything served a purpose only. No need for froufrou.

When I was thirteen or fourteen, I really started to put my foot down, saying I needed to get my hair cut more regularly. Because let me tell you: my features were now growing out of all control, and this crew cut was doing me no favours. I still have sizable features, which I finally grew into, but as a kid, I had the biggest eyes and nose and mouth. Some of these things, to this day, I am still self-conscious about.

My brothers had hit the age where they could get their hair cut more regularly, so I used that against my mum. Eventually, she gave in.

That first "real" haircut was really short at the sides and about an inch long on top. The top part was brushed all the way forward, where it came to little gelled, separated spikes that fell suspended over my forehead. When white guys wore this style, their hair made a fringe that didn't touch their forehead, because they had soft, fine, straight hair. But the only way I could figure out how to get my hair to stick up like that was to spray it and then hold it there with my fingers under-neath. My mum, good woman that she is, would actually stand there and blow-dry it for me *while I held my fingers there*. It was a solid team effort to make me look presentable every morning. I didn't have the face for it, but at the time, I liked it.

Then I started to realize that I needed longer, bigger hair. So I started to do something that was so unwise. I began to sport what I call "the Utah haircut," which is tried and true and still walking around the streets of Utah today.

This is how it goes: The back is spiked up, in fluffy little spikes like a baby chick. The front is sort of swept down across your face. The overall effect looks like you somehow swam to wherever you were going, but then got electrocuted on the way, but the electrocution somehow only affected the back portion of your head. Very much sexy. Very much flattering. Very much should never happen again.

I sported this very ill-advised cut for years, until someone finally had the balls to tell me it was an American lesbian haircut. At the time, I didn't want to out myself—and I certainly didn't want to out myself as a lesbian—so I changed it. And by "changed it," I mean I decided to get rid of the electric shock portion going on in the back of my head and just make it look like I full-on swam from school to my job. My hair was always slightly shiny and slicked across my face, where it remained for seven or eight years.

At some point while I was sporting this style, I decided to switch from gel to pomade and grow out my sideburns. And also straighten them. I had seen the look on a runway show (I wish I could remember which one) and thought it looked really cool and different. I had never seen it before in person . . . for good reason. I was actually wearing it this way—long, straightened sideburns—when I met my husband, Rob.

My hair had always gotten a lot of attention, and I liked that, but it took me a while to understand that sometimes it was negative attention. When I first met Rob, I mistook his surprise at my straightened sideburns to mean he liked them. But of course, "Whoa, your sideburns!" is not synonymous with, "I like your sideburns."

Eventually, I realized that to balance the size of my features, I needed *high hair*. When I was twenty-five, I landed on the pomp, and it has stayed this way ever since. As it's become increasingly grey, it's gotten more interesting. I want to be age-appropriate, but not one of those people who clings desperately to his youth. When I got to my very late twenties and was wearing it "high and tight," I thought, *I can wear my hair this way into my fifties and sixties.* It's a classic style you would have seen fifty years ago. My version is higher than the classic version, but it still harkens back to it. Classic but still current.

As someone who has gone through a hair evolution, I have a lot of feelings about hair. When it comes to hair, there are some trends that need to die.

I know it's teetering off, but that red wash people are wearing needs to stop. I don't mean ginger-coloured hair—that colour is stunning. No, you know the one I'm talking about; it looks like a burgundy red, and no one's hair is actually that colour. Nobody favours this colour. You can agree or disagree, and I don't really care. What I know is that if God didn't create a colour for somebody's hair, then that colour will not do anything for your skin tone. Green or blue or bright red hair is not flattering. Yes, if you choose to dye your hair that colour for a style moment, so be it, and it can be cool. If this is your forever look, though, you might want to reconsider. And if your friends tell you they love it, they just don't want to hurt your feelings. If you're reading this with one of these colours in your hair, I've come too far to take my words back, so I'm going to have to push forward. Let it go.

Another problem is bangs. Pretty much every female friend in my life texts me at some point and says, "Oh my gosh, Tan, I think I want bangs." And I have told them, time and again, that I love bangs but you will regret them in a month when they start to grow out. This is true for everyone, so I'm going to say it once and for all. *You will for sure regret them.* Bangs always suck when they start growing out. I love bangs, but women, you must do your gay friends a favour. The decision to get bangs is yours. Don't put that shit on us. If you want a shoulder to cry on when your hair is going through that awkward growing-out phase, I can't be that person when I was the one who warned you. I love an "I told you so" more than anyone I've ever met. It's my worst quality, for sure.

They will look cute for a few weeks, but you will suffer for the next six months.

Another pet peeve of mine is really long hair. Some women will tell me, "My husband finds this sexy." You can have long hair, but when your hair is hitting your butt, it ceases to be sexy. You look like you just escaped from a cult. Or maybe you didn't even escape the cult; you were sent away from it because even they didn't want to look at that long hair anymore. So just cut it. Mid-back-length is great; any closer to your butt and you've gone too far, kid.

No good has ever come of a man's perm. If your hair is not naturally curly, but you want curls, just know that I'm sorry, but you shouldn't have curls. Life isn't fair, and you can't have everything you want, and it looks like curls are one of those things.

This brings me to gelled hair. I honestly don't know if anything more needs to be said here, so I'm going to say it again, in caps: GELLED HAIR. If you don't know what I mean by that, and you're wearing gel in your hair, then your friends are terrible.

Whether you are a man or a woman, there are many good hairstyles out there. If you are struggling with your hair, ask yourself, *Am*

I doing all I can? If you do not have a blow-dryer, and you are wondering if you should, the answer is yes. Man or woman, if you want a certain hairstyle, you will have to blow-dry it into submission. No one can just shower, towel-dry, walk away, and expect their hair will miraculously become stylish. Hair does not self-style, unless you have perfectly straight or perfectly curly hair, which most of us do not. Those people are the lucky exceptions. We are not those people.

Also, sir, nobody is going to accuse you of being homosexual just because you own a blow-dryer. It will make a huge difference to your appearance. And if they do ask if you're gay after seeing your beautifully turned-out coif, smile and thank them, because someone assuming you are gay is usually their way of saying you are so darn stylish that you must have heightened powers. Own it, bitch; stop being so offended.

While we're on the topic of hair, I think more men should know more about grooming. I hate that men don't really talk about it, and I'd love for it to be less taboo. If you want to look good, why not?

I'm South Asian, and I have a unibrow, so I use tweezers to split that bad boy up and create twinners whose mission in life is to keep their distance. I started plucking when I was probably fourteen or fifteen. I had seen my sisters doing it and didn't think to try anything else. It hurts like a motherfucker the first few times, but you get used to it really quickly. I pluck lightly every few days, so it takes no longer than a minute or so. It's quick, easy, and keeps my shape looking well maintained but natural.

I used to pluck the underside of my brows, too, because I thought people couldn't tell, but I stopped doing that in my twenties because I didn't want to look like a drag queen anymore. No shade to drag queens. That Liza look just wasn't working for me. Now my eyebrows are pretty much their natural shape. Jonathan Van Ness swears I pluck them to within an inch of their life, but I really do not. I love a full brow.

When we started filming, a lot of the boys on the show wanted to change up their look to make it more showbiz-y. But I always want to look like me, so I choose not to participate in hair and makeup before a shoot.

I *hate* wearing makeup. People will sometimes ask what makeup I'm wearing, and the answer is, "I'm not." If I've had a rough night, I'll put a bit of concealer under my eyes, or if I have a blemish, I'll cover it up when filming, but other than that, I just don't wear makeup. I think the boys look fantastic on the show, and makeup works for them, but for me, it just feels like I'm wearing a mask. Also, when I meet people, I want them to see me looking the same as I do on TV, so I like to keep it as natural as I can.

I'm blessed with brown skin, and I don't get blemishes very often. I also take very, very good care of my skin. I'm all about skin-care products, and I'm loyal to a couple of brands in particular that keep my face clean and moisturized.

When I was younger, so many people told me, "Take care of your skin now," and thank gosh I listened. I don't go out in the sun, and I have a face mask I've been using for ten years that works wonders. I once saw an interview with the editor of Korean Vogue and she essentially said that while the magazine promotes many commercial products, what she really uses is this homemade mask. Ever since, I've used this thing a few times a week, and I swear by it.

RECIPE: TAN'S HOMEMADE FACE MASK

Half cup yogurt—I use FAGE 2% fat Greek yogurt
Contents of one green tea bag (steep for one minute in hot
water before emptying the leaves into the yogurt)

1. Mix well, then apply generously to a clean face. Leave
    on for 10 to 12 minutes, then scrape off. Wash face thor-
    oughly with warm water to remove completely, then
    rinse with cold water to close pores. Follow up with your
    regular moisturizer.

WINGS

When I was eighteen, I moved to Manchester for a few years. My family was already moving there to be closer to my mum's family, so I decided to join them. During that brief period of time, I had twenty-four different jobs, some of which I left within a single day.

Here was the problem: I didn't know where I was going in life, but I knew I wanted to make money, obvs. I also wanted power and seniority where it was completely deluded and absolutely not deserved. So I would apply for jobs, I would get them, and then when that didn't work out the way I expected, I would leave.

I was the OG millennial.

I was a very good interviewee. I knew the right things to say, I always turned up in appropriate attire, and I was very peppy and positive. I always showed up in a lovely suit, a tie, and nice shoes. One time, a bunch of candidates were waiting to be called in for their interviews, and one of the other interviewees in the waiting room assumed I was the boss when I walked in. But I knew if I dressed extra, I would get the job. People took me seriously when I dressed seriously.

There were a couple of jobs in particular that I left *immediately*. One job I left on my first lunch break. I had gotten a job selling spa treatments on the street. The job actually paid really, really well. I thought, *I'm a people person! I can do this!* Within an hour, I realized the person I was shadowing was a complete moron and that he was able to make a lot of his sales by being really flirtatious with women. I did not have that skill. Flirting with women was definitely not a thing I excelled at.

I thought, *Oh, shit. Oh, shit, Oh, shit. This is the kind of job for somebody who probably doesn't have any other options.* It didn't seem like the kind of job a kid dreams of having one day, that's for sure. If you have that job and you love it, good for you. It was not the job for me. So a few hours in, I said, "Can I take my lunch break early?" I knew that as soon as I could get away from this, I was going to get out. Then I grabbed my bag, and I never turned up again. I was very resolute about it. I stopped at the grocery store on the way home to get something sweet to treat myself, and then I went home to eat my feelings. The job sucked so hard; I didn't feel remorse about that at all.

They called me many, many times. I did not answer. I'm a terrible person and probably going to hell.

I learned that I never wanted to be a salesperson on the street. I didn't realize how uncomfortable it would be to have to stop randos and try to encourage them to get a spa treatment.

The funny thing is, my main job on *Queer Eye* is to encourage people to take some time to take care of themselves. So now it's come full circle. I got my job training in those few hours on that horrible job. I now tell everyone that they can improve the quality of their lives if they just take the time to pamper themselves a little.

This pattern continued for my next ten or fifteen jobs. One was in a call center, one was at a retail store, one was at the front desk of a medical facility . . . They were fine jobs, but they weren't career options for me. I should have realized this before I ever started those jobs. I should have saved my money and taken the time to figure out what it was I actually wanted to do as a career. But it started to become a sort of challenge, like, *Let me see how many jobs I can get.* See? Straight to hell.

At one point, I got a job as a district manager for a large fashion retailer. I'd been a store manager before, and so I managed to bluff my way into this district manager position. I did it for a couple of weeks, but I loathed my boss so hard. He was the biggest bully and a bad manager, and I cannot abide bad management, especially from somebody I thought wasn't very smart.

One day, I was meant to be flying to Spain to help out with some stores that needed management assistance from the head office crew. But instead, I turned up at the airport and decided, *I can't stand it anymore. I'm out.* Once again, I found myself in a place where I absolutely could not deal with authority. I went to another terminal and decided to purchase a flight to America because I needed a break. I texted my boss, "I'm not coming into work; I'm leaving for America." He texted back, "Are you fucking kidding me? You have to be at work today."

The only regret I have about that one is that I didn't email him, and CC his boss, to tell him that he was the reason I left. He was the reason people kept leaving the company. He was a bully and should never have been put in a position of authority. I should have sent that email so that the person after me wouldn't have to suffer that A-hole.

Anyway, that was the end of that.

Here's my defense: Early on in any job, I knew myself well enough to know that if I hated it then, I would always hate it. Once I've decided I don't like something, it's very difficult for me to turn it around. With every job I'd take, I really did think, *Maybe I can do this! Maybe I'll be happy here.* And then I'd see the environment and culture wasn't right for me and that I could never be there long-term. So why waste time that could be spent trying on another job for size?

When I was twenty-one, I had another retail job for a good year or so, where I had two bosses who were (in my opinion) the most incompetent bullies I'd ever come across. We all worked at the company together, but they worked at the head office and would have to come to conduct store visits and training with me every couple of months. However, they saw their trips to our store as party trips, so they would come in hungover and wouldn't do their job of training me properly yet would be the first ones to scold me if something wasn't done correctly. So I made a complaint to HR. "These people are meant to be training me, and they never show up on time. And if they do show up, they do the bare minimum," I told them. My bosses found out I had made the complaint, and they made my life hell for the next few weeks.

One day, one of them got into a heated argument with me, and I told her, "You are so stupid. You have always been so stupid, and I promise if you take me down, I will take you down with me. I will outsmart you, and you know it." I was very calm. I didn't raise my voice. I was very matter-of-fact about it, and that infuriated her. But I meant it. I wasn't one to be trifled with.

That day came sooner than I'd thought. It was the summertime and the air conditioning in the store was broken. In the UK, legally, if it's above a certain temperature and you don't have air conditioning, you have to close your business down because it's a health concern. It was over thirty-three degrees Celsius (about ninety-one degrees Fahrenheit), and the store was overheating, and so I did what any sensible person would do and I closed down. I tried to call my boss to let her know, but she didn't answer.

The next day, I got a phone call from her. "You closed the store early. This is against company policy, and we're going to have to let you go," she said oh so gleefully. There, she had me. She finally had a reason to fire me, and she was relishing it.

I told her I was following the law, but she didn't care. She said I was fired. It was the only job I've ever been fired from. So I said to her, "Wonderful, if you're firing me, can you please send me a letter explaining why?" She said she would.

Of course, I knew what I was doing. I needed that letter in order to take legal action against her and the company. I had outsmarted her, as I once told her I would.

We had one last HR meeting in order for me to be officially fired. I sat there and listened to her grievances; she basically told me I was the worst employee the world had ever seen as the HR manager (her close friend) sat and took notes while looking at me with a smirk on her face. Finally, I said, "Are we done with this portion of the conversation? I'd like to tell you my part." I told her I was taking legal action against them. "I know you think you're firing me, but I'm going to get you fired," I told her. "What you're doing is actually illegal, and you should have done your research."

She was livid. Livid! "You've always been the most hateful person. You got us to send you something in writing just so you could use it against us!"

And I said, "Yes, because you're both fucking bullies, and you've got your comeuppance. I told you that you were stupid, and you've proven it here today."

I never sued them. In fact, I never even planned on suing them. But I wanted that bully to get what was coming to her. Sure enough, two weeks later, she was out of a job.

Do I regret it? Absolutely not. Do I think it's okay to bully someone at work? No. If you do that, you deserve to lose your job. If I can help take you down, after I've given you multiple warnings that your bullying behaviour won't be tolerated, then all the better. I love an "I told you so" more than anyone I know.

All these jobs taught me how to be the best manager and the best boss that I could be. When you have bad managers, you learn from them and you think, *I'll never do this. I'll never make someone feel like this.* I'm very happy I did all those jobs, and I have no regrets.

I think that when people are in a position of power, they can really affect a person's mental health, happiness, and career. They don't realize what an effect they have on their subordinates. Every action you take truly has an effect on your employees, both at work and outside the office.

One of my favourite jobs was a part-time job as a barman that lasted only one summer. It was at a bar in the gay village in Manchester, on a street where there are about thirty or so gay bars. This was a wine bar with jazz music and an affluent clientele. It wasn't a clubby bar; it was the kind of place you'd go to have a nice drink and a chat with friends.

I didn't drink alcohol at the time—in fact, at the time, I hadn't even tasted alcohol—but I was the highest earner at the bar because people found me (and my complete incompetence) charming. I got more tips than any other bartender, but the reason was because I had no idea what they wanted. I'd say, "You point to what you want, and I'll go get it!" Then I'd ask, "How much of this do you want? How much of that should I pour?" They were making their own drinks. And of course, I would always over-pour. I should have been fired, but everyone thought it was so cute, so I continued to collect high tips for us all to pool and benefit from at the end of the shift.

I loved that job, but I quit that one, too. In fact, I quit one day with no notice. Gosh, I really was just the worst when it came to leaving a job. I should really work on that.

Anyway, I was working during Manchester Pride, the village's annual gay pride event, and I had never been to pride before. Everyone was having so much fun, and the streets of the village were packed.

There were so many people everywhere, you couldn't move. My friends were like, "How are you working? Let's do this!" I was suffering the worst FOMO, so I turned to my boss and said, "I'm sorry. I quit. I'm so sorry." Then I jumped over the bar and left. Total dick move. Don't hate me for it. I was young and just wanted to live my best gay life that weekend. Ugh.

I lived it up for the weekend, and then I never went back.

Of all the jobs I've left, that is the one I feel the worst about. If I could contact them now and say I'm so sorry, I would. That was totally shitty, I know. But if there are any gays out there reading this, you'll understand all too well. Your first pride is a big deal.

Perhaps the craziest job I had was the time I was a flight attendant. It was meant to be a six-month seasonal job, but I only lasted two months. Here's how convincing I was in an interview: I managed to get the job with absolutely no experience. I had no right to be there, but I sold myself well. And so, I managed to get the only flight attendant job I'd ever applied for.

I wanted to travel but didn't have the funds to travel, and I thought, *I'm going to do this. It can't be that difficult. All they're doing is serving tea and coffee and a bit of something else.* I was about nineteen at the time. Obviously, I had no idea what was actually involved.

Being a flight attendant is no joke. They do not get the credit they deserve. The thirty-day training included some of the hardest moments of my life. It was very difficult, and many people failed. I have a very, very, very good memory—all throughout school, I could just read something once and get a good grade on the exam. For this job, I studied and studied and even then only scraped by. The safety texts were just so freaking complicated.

I thought it was going to be super glamorous. It was not. I felt like a glorified waiter. Having to open the trash chute and tidy up the restrooms on a long-haul flight, well, there was nothing glamorous about it.

The least glamorous thing of all was that I got assigned to many flights from England to Spain. In England, we call it the eighteen-to-thirty crowd, which in America is kind of like the spring breakers. The passengers were often drunk, and when they were drunk, they weren't concerned about censoring racism. This was a couple of years after 9/11, and they had no qualms about openly referring to my people as *terrorists*. The flight would start off well enough, but by the end of the flight, it would be clear they weren't so happy that I was the one serving them.

I remember my last day very distinctly. It was a flight back to England from Ibiza, and this bunch of rowdy people were being aggressive. They wanted more alcohol; they were really forceful about it. I didn't know how to deal with men in particular who were drunk and who wanted more alcohol.

At one point, they got super angry and started asking for coffee because I wouldn't give them alcohol anymore. Because they had been so rude to me the whole time, I finally barked back, "Get your own fucking coffee." I walked back to the galley (which is at the back of the plane) and said to the main flight attendant, "I quit. I'm not putting up with this anymore."

The moment the plane was parked, I walked off and handed in my wings—which is the little badge they give you—and didn't go back to work there ever again.

Being a flight attendant is tough because people take out their aggression on you. You're the face of the business and also the front line. If something's not right, they're angry at you. It's incredibly difficult to manage in a confined space. I have mad respect for flight attendants for putting up with so much.

Of course, sometimes, leaving these jobs, I didn't feel guilty. This was particularly true when the people I worked for were horrible and they didn't seem to be decent, kind folks. But the majority of the time, I would feel such guilt. I'd think, *They hired me when they could have hired somebody else.* But the guilt was never enough to make me stay. I knew that once I had made up my mind about a job, it could never be turned around.

If I hadn't built a personal connection, I was less apologetic. If I liked the people and they seemed great, I would stick around. I stayed at a data entry job where the people were lovely for much longer than I should have because I felt like an integral part of the team. If ever I built a relationship, I would feel real guilt about leaving them.

Would I go back and do it all again? Absolutely not. I wish I had the knowledge as a twenty-three-year-old to say, "Save the money from the job you have and take the time to think about what you want to do, as opposed to job hunting out of desperation because you just need a paycheck."

Even though I truly had over thirty jobs between the ages of sixteen and twenty-seven (which is when I started my business), I only listed three jobs on my résumé. I included the ones where I did well and had stayed for over a year. To address the gaps, I would explain that I was traveling and going to the school of life. No, I didn't ever really say *school of life*, but could you imagine if I did?

You have to lie on your résumé, right? Everyone does it. I was just highlighting the best parts of my career. *Besides*, I thought, *just because I quit a lot of jobs doesn't mean I won't be good at* this *job!*

Moral of the story: you just never know what you're getting when you hire Tan France.

SLIPPERS

When I was twenty-five, I visited Salt Lake City on vacation. I had been going there regularly for a couple of years after initially visiting on a trip with my co-worker, who'd convinced me to come check out his home state. The very first evening, as I sat there at a Chili's, I said to him, "I'm going to make this my home one day." He thought I was joking. I wasn't.

The city was gorgeous, and the people were so, so friendly, I knew that I eventually wanted to call this place home. Don't ask me why . . . unless you seriously want a very long, drawn-out love letter to Salt Lake

City, which I've composed in my head over the last decade or so. The short of it is that the city is beautiful, surrounded by mountains, and the people are incredibly friendly and made me feel more welcome than I'd ever felt before (and they continue to do so). It's my happy place. So along the way, I made it my goal to make a few friends there.

It was January of 2008, and whenever I'd go out to bars and clubs with my Utah friends, they would get frustrated that the people they were attracted to would flirt with me because I was the only brown British person in town and quite possibly in the whole state of Utah. "I've been trying to get with this person for so long," they would whine, "and you just roll in and take them."

So they decided to do a little experiment. They set me up with a profile on Connexion, which was like a gay version of Facebook. It wasn't like the apps we have now—you would never dream of sending someone an inappropriate photo. It was meant for making friends and actually dating-dating. "With just your photo, they won't know you have an accent!" they said, which is basically saying I'm not attractive enough without my British accent, thankyouverymuch. Like, ew. So rude. They clearly weren't the best of friends to me, and if you're wondering if they're still around, the answer is a hell no. They were more fair-weather, club friends, it turns out. I can't really judge them for it, as we were all in our early twenties and out to have a good time. They were all native Utahns, born and bred, and so to have an "exotic" friend worked well for them in the small gay community.

Am I maybe a little bitter that they assumed that the only way I could get a guy was by using my most extra version of my accent? Yep. Do I need to get over it and realize we were kids and they were probably too drunk to realize they were being hurtful? Uh-huh.

So anyway, they put me on this site, and that first day, I got a few messages. Rob was one of them. His line was, "You don't look like you're from around here," to which I replied, "No shit, Sherlock." And then we got into a light conversation. My sassy side really worked for me, it seems.

What I did not realize at the time is that he hadn't had much exposure to people of colour, having only lived in Utah and Wyoming, and he assumed I was Mexican. Now, calm down, you crazy liberals. No, he is not a big fat racist. He just didn't think for a second that a South Asian guy from the UK would have chosen Salt Lake City as a vacation destination. But, also, yeah, it was all looks-based and clearly that twat saw all of us brownies as the same . . . Mexican. Burn that bitch at the stake!

We continued to chat, but I didn't tell him I was from the UK.

After chatting for a few days, he asked if we could go out. I said we could have lunch, because lunch isn't really a date. It's perfectly non-committal. I also told him I would like to go to the Olive Garden.

Bear with me on this one.

On the show *Will & Grace* (which I was obsessed with in high school), Will and Grace are friends with a couple named Rob and Ellen, whose only attributes are that they are very, very boring. Rob and Ellen always want to get dinner at a place called the Olive Garden, which Will and Grace find frightfully dull. I had never been to an Olive Garden, but this seemed like a good test. If this person could keep me entertained in what was apparently the most boring place in the world, then I would be highly impressed.

The day of our lunch arrived, and I put on an outfit I liked and felt comfortable in. It was classic and simple. Slim-cut indigo jeans.

Fitted grey cashmere sweater. Beautiful dark brown shoes and a killer black knee-length trench that fit to perfection.

Rob got out of his truck—because he's a good rancher's son—and he had this look on his face like, *Oh, shit. He's not Mexican.*

I looked at him and saw he was wearing . . . slippers. They were shearling lined, brown leather, and they were very, very nice around-the-house slippers, but they were not appropriate for a date. In his defense, they were actually not house slippers. They were designed to be worn out and about, as a fashionable, comfortable shoe. Did I care for them any more after learning this? No.

Slippers aside, he had this quirky style I really appreciated. I had seen on his Connexion profile that he'd wear these slightly shiny '70s printed shirts, which he would tuck into his nicely fitted jeans. It was weird, but just seeing that, I could tell he had personality and that he was making an effort. He didn't want to be a basic bitch. He liked to stand out from the crowd and experiment with style, which I really gravitated toward.

The Olive Garden, on the other hand, was exactly what I'd pictured. I don't know if I had an image in mind of what it would look like, but as soon as I walked in, I thought, *This feels right.* How else would it be decorated? The walls were covered in Venetian plaster, and the chairs had wheels on the bottom. I thought, *Oh god, this is what they think Italy looks like.* And then I thought, *The person who created this has obviously never been to Italy, or even Little Italy in New York.* The food I had tasted of nothing.

Since then, however, I've discovered that the Olive Garden has one of my favourite meals. Mind you, it's not Italian food; they fired fast and loose with that phrasing. But they have Alfredo sauce, and their breadsticks are killer. If you are forced to go to the Olive Garden, get the breadsticks and the Alfredo sauce. It's salty, it's carb-y, it has so many calories—but it is truly incredible.

The best thing about the Olive Garden is that when you arrive, they always ask, "Are you celebrating anything today?" The question they should ask is, "What happened to your life that you're ending up at the Olive Garden? What ailment are these breadsticks and Alfredo sauce attempting to cure?" Please know: I am throwing no shade at anybody who's thinking, *That's all I can afford.* Because let me tell you, Olive Garden ain't cheap. I swear to Lucifer, you can go to a real Italian restaurant and you'll pay less than you would at the Olive Garden, and for something more authentic. I'd rather you go to the Cheesecake Factory. At least they know what they are.

Anyway, back to the date. At the time, Rob was very newly out, at the tender age of thirty, and hadn't been on many gay dates before. Anyone who really knows me knows that I could talk to a brick wall for hours and hours before I realize it hasn't said a word back. So I was sitting at the table like, "Chat, chat, chat," and he was blushing the whole time. He went to the restroom a couple of times, which I later found out was so that he could calm himself down. I know, man. Swoon.

We started wrapping up our lunch, but we weren't ready to say goodbye yet. We agreed that we should continue on with the date, which I hadn't expected I'd want to do, at all, as I had never had a date that I wanted to extend and which also involved a location change. I said I would happily see a movie with him. We headed over to the cinema and planned to watch whatever was playing next. Unfortunately, the only thing playing was *Bride Wars*, quite possibly the worst movie ever, starring Kate Hudson and Anne Hathaway. I love the two actresses, and lord knows I love a rom-com, but that was a tough pill to swallow on a first date.

At the cinema, he leaned over to get his glasses from his bag, and I touched him lightly on his back. He turned to me and said, "You like me?" I simply smiled back at him.

We held hands as we watched the movie, and when it was over, I still didn't want it to end. So, we got coffee, and finally—six hours later—I said I had dinner plans. He insisted on driving me back to where I was staying. It was the perfect first date.

During this date, I learned that, up until that point in his life, Rob was Mormon. I didn't really understand what Mormons were all about. Before I came to Utah, I assumed they were the same as the Amish. I was very, very much mistaken. Rob told me that he didn't drink alcohol, and I wanted to sing hallelujah from the *fucking rooftop*. I had always thought that if you date a white guy, he's going to be a drinker. Growing up in England, I'd never met a person outside of my own community who didn't drink . . . a lot. I had always disliked drinking and the way it made me feel, and I assumed that was just my lot in life. I'd have to put up with it if I wanted to keep a partner. So, the fact that there was a whole bunch of people out here in this (magical-freaking-Eden) state blew my mind. That nugget of information alone brought Rob to the front of the dating pack.

He texted me right away, which I loved. (I hate those fucking games. If you like someone, text them.) "Do you want to hang out tomorrow?" he asked. He worked at a children's hospital, where he got one thirty-minute break during his twelve-hour shift. And during his break, he drove the ten minutes to come see me. He made sure he saw me every day that week, until it was time for me to head back home to England.

We had only been seeing each other for a week, and as we were saying goodbye, he said, "I think this is the worst thing you can say, but I think I'm falling in love with you."

I was like, "Oh, shit. I'm on vacation and I'm about to go back home. I really like you, too, but I can't say that yet." I didn't know if I truly felt that or if I was caught up in the holiday romance, and I didn't want to say it unless I could legit back it up. So, I didn't say it back.

He wore a necklace that I thought was just lovely: a simple chain with a coin hanging from it. He gave me his necklace and said, "I know if I give this to you, you'll see me again one day, to return it to me."

The whole flight home, I kept thinking, *I like this guy so much. Why can't this work?* As soon as I got back, I told him that if he wanted to come to the UK, we could spend some more time together. And a month later, he came to visit me for ten days.

I was living in Manchester at the time, but I wanted Rob to see London, as it's one of my very favourite cities. As soon as Rob arrived, I felt so connected to him. I felt so much love for him that when we arrived at our hotel, I told him that I was falling in love with him, too. That set the tone for the rest of his trip. We were young and in love and at the start of what was to be a wicked holiday.

I showed him around London for a few days, and then we went on to Tenerife (a small Spanish island off the coast of northwest Africa). While we were in London, I introduced him to some of my best friends—the Ali sisters—from the north of England. We went for dinner, and during that time, Rob smiled and nodded as I looked on knowing full well he hadn't a darn clue what the heck my friends were saying. They're from Leeds and have the strongest Leeds accents, but Rob was so sweet and only once leaned over to me to say that he had no idea what they were talking about. My friends loved him instantly.

It was Rob's first trip to Europe, so every sight we saw blew him away. It was lovely to see the city through the eyes of a newbie. I so wanted him to extend his stay, as ten days just didn't seem long enough, but by the end of his trip he was exhausted and needed to feel normal again, so he went back home. I missed him immediately.

Before he left, he said, "I'm positive you're my person."

To which I replied, "I'm positive you're my person, too."

Rob went back to America, but the following month, I decided I was going to go to America for three months to try to live with him. When I look back on it now, it's insane that only after two months of dating I would want to live with him. But it made perfect sense to me at the time. I got a work visa, and we lived together on and off for the next two years. It was bliss. Every three months my visa would expire, and I'd have to go home. Our relationship continued that way; three months together, six months long distance, on and off for another four years.

To anyone who is currently in a long-distance relationship or who is considering it, if you want it to work, it can. From the first week we met, whenever Rob and I were apart, we would communicate for two or three hours a day, seven days a week, via Skype. When you're long distance, the emotional connection is very strong because you take the physical aspect out of it. All you can do is connect emotionally. We got to know each other very, very well. In a way, it's why ten years later it still feels like we're in the honeymoon stage.

TAN'S FIRST
DATE DOS AND DON'TS

DO

- Be showered, deodorized, and spritzed. Fresh as a daisy.

DON'T

- Go with natural deodorant. Don't think for a second that that shit will cut it. It won't!

DO

- Pick an outfit you feel your best in. I wore an outfit that I'd worn before, and that gave me the confidence boost I needed.

DON'T

- Overdo the look. Make sure the outfit is appropriate for the venue of your date. You don't want to come across as too try-hard.

DO

- Be on time to the date. I was ready to go.

DON'T

- Be late because you think that gives you the power. That, in fact, makes you a douche!

DO

- Be engaging and light-hearted.

DON'T

- Talk about how much you hate your ex / job / best friend / mum / cat.

DO

- Convey confidence. I wanted Rob to see that I had my

shit together, or at least was on my way to having my shit together.

DON'T

- Be too self-deprecating or too arrogant. It's a fine balance, but one that can tip against you if you're not careful.

DO

- Offer to pay the bill! This is important, whatever sex you are. It's good manners, whether you end up paying or not.

DON'T

- Just expect the other person to pay, without offering. You do not want to seem entitled.

DO

- Communicate. I texted Rob shortly after the date to thank him, even though I hadn't yet made up my mind if I was going to actively pursue it. It was the kind thing to do!

DON'T

- Play that lame-ass game of waiting three days to text or

for the other person to text first. You don't want to be the reason you're still single. And, lemme tell you, these kinds of games will ensure that you are!

DO

- Be yourself. I was myself with Rob. I let him see the real, true me!

DON'T

- Catfish that bitch. They will see the real you eventually. May as well be yourself from the get-go.

After following these rules, Rob and I continued to have many successful dates, which turned into marriage. Ten years later, we still play by these dos and don'ts.

PSA: SIGNAL YOUR INTENTIONS

One thing I say regularly in my life is "Signal your intentions." How is anyone supposed to know what's going on unless you signal your intentions? This is especially true in dating.

After our date, Rob texted me almost immediately afterward telling me what a lovely time he had, and I immediately reciprocated to tell him how much I enjoyed the date and how I wanted to see him again. One thing that infuriates me is when people play this game, like, "I can't text you too soon!" Or "I should wait a day!" Or "But *he* should text *me!*" Get the fuck over that. If you're going down that path, you're in for a shitty, shitty time. You could get six months in and discover you're just playing a part in a game with a person you don't even know.

If I like someone, I'm going to say, "I like you, and I'd like to see you again." If they get freaked out, that's on them. Don't get me wrong;

if you declare your undying love right off the bat, that's a problem. But if they aren't willing to match your excitement, that is not your person. Move the fuck on. Next!

I think signaling your intentions is something you need to do early on. Many people disagree, but the notion of declaring exclusivity is something I've never understood. If I'm dating someone, I'm dating them. We are exclusive until I tell them I don't want to be with them anymore. I don't want to make out with someone who wants to make out with everyone else. I think there should be a universal rule that if you're intimate with someone, maybe just keep it in your pants.

If you're just casually seeing someone out and about and that works for you, that's okay. But that is not dating.

Another thing I hear a lot is "I met this guy, and he's great, but . . ." This irks me more than anything in the world. It's usually followed by something like, "I don't like his style, so I'm going to encourage him to dress like this . . ." or "I don't like his job, so I'm going to encourage him to do something else . . ." No. Wrong. You can't change him. You're not that formidable. And he may be happy exactly the way he is.

If you want to change that much of a person, they're not your fucking person. This is especially true if the thing you want to change is a fundamental thing, like if the person doesn't believe in marriage, or doesn't want kids, or doesn't share your religion. Your beauty and your humor will not convince him that there is a God. Next!

COWBOY BOOTS

When I first met Rob, he was wearing slippers. Perhaps it's not surprising, then, that I started buying Rob clothes within the first few months we knew each other. It wasn't to change his style, necessarily. I actually really liked his quirky, individual style, and I've never wanted to change that. I obviously like to shop for clothes, and I liked buying him nice things. I loved spoiling him. He had mostly been buying clothes from thrift stores and wanted to look like he was making more of an effort to look refined. Since he said he wanted help, I was happy to provide it.

But here's the thing about Rob. For years, he would tell me he wanted my advice, because I was more comfortable with style. But giving your partner advice is difficult, especially when your partner is Rob France. He would ask me what I thought of something he was wearing, and then when I gave him my opinion, he would throw a strop and get kind of moody. These were the only times we ever really fought. It was all so stupid.

Eventually, we had to sit down and have a come-to-Muslim-Jesus moment, where I said, "Do you want my advice, or do you not want my advice?"

I realized part of the problem was that he would have already owned and worn something for a while, and then I would tell him I didn't like it. To say "You've already bought something, and now I'm going to criticize it" doesn't help anybody. By that point, it was too late. So what I started to do—and I still do this with him and my friends—is to go shopping with him instead. Then, you can give your opinion about something when they haven't spent the money on it yet. It's amazing what a difference that makes in the reaction it receives. When they haven't already parted with the cash—and decided on all the ways they'll wear that troublesome item—that's the time to say, "Maybe that's not the option for you. Let's continue on the hunt."

I also offered to go through his closet with him and tell him which things were working and which things were not. There weren't a lot of things that he couldn't make work, but every now and then, when left to shop on his own, he would go for loud pieces. Statement pieces. The problem with that was that they were hard to style, as they were bold for him. So they'd inevitably take up prime real estate in the closet and never see the light of day. Like the wool winter coat with the dramatic fur collar. Where was my Wyoming husband going to wear this coat in Utah, and for what occasion?

This process of working through his closet was way better than telling him to change before we were headed for a night out, which would only hurt his feelings. Again, I *never* offered my unsolicited opinion on his style. It was only ever after he asked me what I thought, and honestly, the only times he asked me were when I could tell he knew the outfit wasn't working for him.

Back then, Rob would hold on to special-occasion clothes for a wedding or a birthday party or a nice dinner date. He'd look great in them, but you'd only see them every three months. One day, I said, "Why do you hang on to special-occasion clothes that you could be using every day to make every day feel like a special occasion?"

The same is true for everybody. Let them out! Don't you want to feel great every day? I'm not saying to wear a ball gown every day, but if you have some nicer pieces, there's nothing wrong with wearing them more often. It's never made sense to me to keep shut away in a closet the items that make you feel attractive and look your best. Why save that feeling for once every few weeks? Buy more of those kinds of pieces and work them into your everyday wardrobe so you can feel that pep in your step way more often.

I would also make a point to compliment him when he wore something I loved, and just not comment if he wore something I didn't. Now Rob is stylish all on his own, but I'll go through the same process with my friends, and I find that's the best way to give my opinion on someone's wardrobe if I know they're struggling with it. I compliment when it's great, and I don't when it's not. This process is tried and true and seems to have caused as little conflict as possible.

One thing Rob does that drives me insane—it's the only thing that drives me insane about him—is that he always wants to dress in the same style as I do. I'll wear something, and then a few weeks later, he'll wear something identical. He will have purchased something in order to be my twin. I told him, "I don't love anything less than having my partner look like my white twin." But he hasn't stopped yet.

Still, I'll wear something I love, and a couple of weeks later, he'll emerge from the closet wearing the exact same outfit, and then I can't wear it again. He says I work in the fashion industry, so I should be the one to come up with something new. "If I want to wear what you're wearing, that means you've done your job well."

So now I've been forced to go into styles that I know there's no way he'll wear. There are some things that white middle-aged guys can't get away with. It's kind of like how Asian girls can get away with things that would look batshit crazy on a white girl. That's the only way I can keep him off me.

There is one thing, though, that you'll never see me wear. Since those early days of dating, I made it very clear that cowboy boots have a place, and that place is on a ranch. (Side note to my in-laws— you live in Wyoming, so you get a pass.) Unless you are actually a rancher, you should not be wearing cowboy boots.

I know cowboy boots come in and out of style. If they're peppered into your wardrobe every now and then, so be it. But if that's all you have in your closet, you should probably reevaluate. Cowboy boots, even when a trend, are not everyday footwear.

Further side note: I also feel a weird sense of cultural appropriation when I consider wearing cowboy boots, which is another reason I don't think this South Asian guy needs them in his life.

ODE TO A ONE-PIECE

I think when people go to college for fashion, a lot of them assume they'll be the next Alexander McQueen or Stella McCartney or whomever they might love. But I learned early on that those people are really the exception. They're one in a million.

Because I didn't want to be a starving artist designer, my plan was always to create a mass apparel brand. (I take umbrage at the fact that most colleges don't teach you how to work for a brand like, say, Topshop. In fact, I thought once I retired, I might like to teach students how to become apparel designers for a brand as opposed to being a fashion designer. But of course that didn't happen, because now I'm on a show.) I knew I would have to learn on the job, so I started taking jobs where I would learn technical design and what we call *tech packs*, because I knew that's what I'd need to go into mass production—I couldn't just drape something on a mannequin and be able to produce it for the masses in a size XS through XL.

So I went with my gut, and I started working for brands that could teach me. I decided I'd learn as many facets of these apparel brands as I could. I worked for Selfridges, I worked for Zara, I learned how to run a store, how to visually merchandise, how to order product in. Finally, I worked for an American brand called Shade Clothing, which was a modest clothing business catering to Mormon women. It was a niche market and incredibly successful. It was also a smaller company, which meant everyone who worked there wore a number of hats. I started out as the regional manager, but right away they realized I was overqualified, so I became the director of sales and operations. I oversaw everything from design to production to retail.

Shade was successful, and the company was sold to a private buyer in my second year working for them, which meant I was out of a job. At the time, I was on a work visa, and if I wasn't employed, it meant I would have to leave the country. I couldn't find a new job in time, because there weren't many apparel brands based in Utah—*shock shock horror horror*. And I couldn't use my marriage to a man to stay, because there was no US law that recognized our UK marriage. So I had to find another way.

At that time, I was twenty-six, and I hadn't planned on starting my own company until I turned at least thirty. But I knew that if you had a successful business, with employees and a certain amount of money, you could get a green card. And so I thought, *I guess I'm starting my business earlier than I expected!* I had about $20,000 in savings to put into this business, which isn't a lot when you're talking about launching an apparel brand, but I knew that I could produce a certain amount of product and make it work.

Since Shade had been sold and there was a gap in the market, I decided to start another modest clothing company. I wanted to create something that was more stylish, so the pieces would be cool, commercial clothes that just so happened to cover the parts of the body that Mormon women had to cover.

There were a couple of businesses already making modest clothing, but in my opinion, none of them were stylish enough. So I designed a small collection and stupidly decided I was going to launch my business, Kingdom & State, in England, since that was where I was at the time, and I couldn't figure out how to make an online store and ship. I designed an eighteen-piece collection, then went to China and sewed the samples. Then I took a six-month lease on a store.

We opened the store, and sales were really tough. It just wasn't the right market for what we were selling. We made decent enough money to get by, but the overhead with a store was so high that we couldn't stay afloat. We closed down the store as soon as the six-month lease was up, with a lot of inventory. It was a rough blow for me, but I was determined to make it work. I knew the issue was the location, and that was a problem I was sure I could solve. My product was designed for the US market. I was designing product for Mormon women's coverage requirements, and the mecca for that was the US, and Utah in particular. That would be my initial market before I could expand to the rest of the US.

I hated the modest swimwear that was available at the time. I had saved a vintage picture on Pinterest of a woman in a high-waisted swimsuit, and I thought, *You haven't seen that since the '50s and '60s.* The only version I could find was by Dolce & Gabbana and cost a fortune. I figured I could design an accessible version of that, and I was sure that the Mormon crowd would be all about it. But it would also appeal to non-Mormon women who just wanted more coverage.

So I made my first collection of swimwear—eight swimsuits, six one-pieces and two two-pieces. They were all vintage inspired, harkening back to the '50s. The one-pieces were similar to the iconic crème one-piece that Marilyn Monroe wore. The two-pieces were simple high-waisted bottoms with a structured front panel for extra support, and the top was a mid-length bustier with straps. Designing swimwear is very different from designing clothes, but I learned quickly. The entire collection was around seven hundred pieces, as that was all I could afford to make. It was a tiny collection, but a strong one.

I gave one of my swimsuits to a blogger I'd known through Instagram and asked if she would consider posting it if she liked it. She did, and she did.

When the collection launched, I was boarding a flight to China, where I was going to sample the new collection. I had designed a fall apparel collection, and I was going to have it sampled, which is the process you go through to prepare to go into production, in the event the swim line sold well. Unbeknownst to me, the blogger posted about the swimwear while I was on the plane. By the time my flight landed seventeen hours later, I had sold out—every last one of the seven hundred pieces.

As the Wi-Fi didn't work over the ocean, I only started to get a signal as the plane was really close to landing. As we were about to land, I saw the text from Rob saying, "Oh my god, we sold out." I thought it was a joke, and I replied, "Hahahahaha." But then he responded, "Legit, we sold out. We don't have one piece left."

I was in complete shock. I needed to talk to him on the phone. Yet when we landed, I still couldn't call, because China is really strict when it comes to using phones in the airport. Instagram is also banned in China, so I wasn't able to see if anyone had tagged a photo of the swimsuit.

This was only my second time in China, but I knew that the customs line was very long, and I wouldn't be able to talk to him until I got through it. I was standing on the line for over an hour, tapping my feet and biting my nails (which I've done since I was a little boy). I was so anxious I wanted to scream, which of course I could not do, because I am brown.

There are two things a brown person cannot do, and those are to scream or run through an airport with a backpack on. We struggle to catch flights, too. But we're not allowed to run, because that would alarm all the white people.

So there I was, standing in the airport, screaming in my head. Then, finally, I got into the cab and called him.

"What the fuck are you talking about?" I said. "There is no way we sold out."

He assured me that we had.

I still didn't understand how this was possible. Everything had sold out while I was on the plane? That's a lot to sell through a tiny, tiny website.

"How did this happen?" I asked him.

He said, "I don't know! I woke up, and everything had sold." He said it had been nonstop for a few hours.

"Was there a glitch in the system?"

"No," he assured me. "Every order has a different name on it. People are asking for preorders and when we think we'll get more in."

I immediately called my factory and asked them if we could rush another order, and they said they could do it in six weeks. So we immediately put the collection back online, with a message that said, "Preorder available, back in six weeks." And we continued to sell and sell.

At this point, I called Rob and said, "Now, all on your own, you have to go through all three thousand boxes and send out all three thousand orders."

He is an angel.

I told him he could call some of our friends and ask for help, and he said, "No, we're not the kind of people who ask everyone for help." And for five or six days, he was doing it all himself, around the clock. He fulfilled orders from the time he woke until the time he went to bed.

Mind you, these were massive boxes, and they were all in our tiny one-bedroom apartment. At the time, our living room was no longer a living room; it was a storage space. Our apartment had basically become an office and warehouse that we just so happened to have a bed in. It continued that way for a year and half, with Rob shipping out orders until we could afford to get an office space.

The business was finally working, and I was overjoyed.

When I flew back to America, I brought my new autumn samples with me and started taking them to stores in Utah and Idaho. I would go from store to store with a suitcase and start taking wholesale orders.

It was such a cowboy operation—it's not how it should be done, but it was the only way I knew.

With the money from my wholesale endeavors, I was able to afford to rent a booth at my first trade show, called Magic, in Las Vegas. It's the biggest apparel trade show in the US and attracts a massive number of buyers. I was panicking over the $10,000 fee, but I made back the money on the first day of the show. I did another show—this one a swimwear show—in California, and the likes of Forever 21 and Mod-Cloth purchased my line. They placed large orders for many of the styles I designed that were put into mass production to be sold at their stores and online only three months later. I couldn't quite believe it. The business was finally becoming a real brand.

We went into mass production immediately. Their orders were huge, and I didn't know how I would be able to afford it. I took out financing to make it work. It sold so well that they quadrupled the size of their orders within weeks of the items going online.

Once the swimwear did well, the retailers started ordering apparel, too. My business had become something I'd hoped for but didn't expect to have for many, many years.

For the first two years, I was the only employee of my business. I pretended to have a business address, but it was really our tiny one-bedroom home. Rob shipped all the orders from our living room. I created different email accounts for a payroll manager, a customer service manager . . . I didn't want retailers thinking we were a tiny business. I wanted them to continue to order on the faith that we had this whole team working to get their orders out to them. Over email, I was Jane . . . I was Avery . . . I was Christine . . . I was *so many women*. Whenever they'd ask to speak, I would say we had to correspond by email so there would be a paper trail. I made up ludicrous stories to keep the illusion going. It worked.

For the first two and a half years, we weren't earning much. Everything we made had to go right back into the company—so in addition to running the business, I had to have a job. I was back in the UK because I still didn't have a US work visa, so I had to run the business remotely as Rob continued to take care of shipping on his days off from his regular job.

I had gone from earning a good salary as a director at Shade to working for minimum wage as a temp at a law firm or a mental health clinic or whatever other temp job I could find. I would temp five or six days a week, from 8:00 a.m. until 4:00 p.m. Then I would haul ass and do production and customer service in the evenings, which was when the US was up and at 'em. It was so fucking stressful, and I can't tell you the number of times I broke down, cried, and wanted to quit. It was easily the hardest period of my life.

Although my jobs were temporary, they were still work. I would have the stress of my day job, but all the while I would be worrying about a screwup at the factory, where an item had been produced in mustard instead of a bright yellow, and thinking that if I can't put a spin on this with the buyers, I'll be stuck with over ten thousand dollars' worth of product I can't sell (since factories are notorious about getting off the hook for errors with production), and how I can't afford that kind of hit, so I'd better get on the phone and email ASAP to try to make this all work.

I was sure that a time would come where the business would grow to a point where we could hire a team to help and could reap the rewards.

After two and a half years, I could afford to pay myself. I started to focus on the business full-time and push social media more regularly. However, I was still wise enough to keep my team small. At first, we hired two people and then three. I'd seen—and worked for—so many companies where they employed a bunch of people who spent half the day chilling online. So I made sure I hired people who knew what needed to be done and that their days were full, wearing many, many hats.

Then I had the harebrained idea of creating more businesses. Why not create more clothing brands and just call them different names? At this point, my swimwear had become such a thing that local businesses were starting to pop up and knock me off. There were new businesses popping up all the time that were making pieces that were just like what I'd been doing years before. There was no innovation. Just replicate and rebrand. It was infuriating but completely legal. And, if there's one thing that Utah businesspeople do well, it's copying someone else's work and claiming it as their own.

Utahns, you know I love you, but you fuckwits who knocked me off, you know who you are.

So I thought, *If everyone is knocking me off and becoming successful doing it, then I'll knock myself off.* I started using cheaper fabric and selling my own designs at a much lower price point, and it sold really well. I had a premium brand and a knockoff of my premium brand, and no one knew that both of them were me. It worked so well.

High-waisted two-pieces became massive for me. I also saw the tides were turning and that one-pieces were becoming more and more popular. People were starting to see them not as dowdy and grandma-like but as chic and sophisticated. So while everyone was busy knocking off my two-pieces, I started to make one-pieces that, while modest, were as sexy as they could be and looked like nothing anyone else was doing. The two-piece may have created my business, but the one-piece saved my business. The one-piece created everything I have now.

I love a one-piece bathing suit on a woman. I think women look sexier when they're not showing it all off. If you wear a high-waisted bottom or a one-piece, it looks sexy and sophisticated and chic as fuck. A thong may be good for tanning, but your butt is literally eating that back piece. That's not a great look. And you'll feel so much more confident strolling around knowing your ass isn't eating your swimsuit and your boobs are supported. A bikini is a vulnerable state to be in, and that's maybe not how you want to get your next hot boyfriend.

The '80s ruined us. If you're thirsty for attention, you do you, bish, but if what you want is to feel good about yourself and feel comfortable and supported, wear a one-piece.

Dress for other women. This is as true on the beach as anywhere else. If you're dressing for yourself and other women at the beach, then you're doing something right.

Men, I have some advice for you, too. Let the board shorts die unless you actually own a surfboard. Even then, I'm not sure it's great to surf in them. Board shorts look frumpy—there is nothing cool or sexy about them. My plea to every man out there is this: invest in a pair of shorts that hit your mid-thigh, which will make you look taller and leaner.

LITTLE PINK DRESS

After my businesses were up and running, I started to work with a woman called Rachel Parcell, who runs the blog *Pink Peonies*. I met Rach a few years prior, as she often wore my designs to New York Fashion Week and had helped promote my swimwear. She was killing it with her fashion and lifestyle blog, and even though she was only in her early twenties, women across the world were looking to her for all things lifestyle.

Rachel is incredibly creative and has a very feminine aesthetic, which helped her carve out a niche in this crazy blogging world. With two kids, a husband, and a multimillion-dollar home to boot, she'd become the go-to blogger. One cold, Christmassy day, she asked if I wanted to help her create a brand.

Side note: Before I started working with bloggers, I had some real disdain for them. Over the years, there were literally hundreds, if not thousands, popping up every day, taking selfies and pics of their avocado toast. I never would have thought I'd associate myself with that self-indulgent bunch. However, it took getting to know just one of them to change my opinion.

I know bloggers can seem vapid to the skeptical eye. However, I've come to realize that bloggers are some of the most innovative marketers out there. They bust their balls building up an audience of the most engaged followers. Yes, they do many a sponsored post, but why the heck was I expecting otherwise? They're influencers, and this is how they earn a living. They've managed to carve out a whole, massively profitable industry that gives them freedom to create some amazing content while providing for their families. I've drastically changed my opinion of this savvy bunch.

Do I still want to hammer-punch their brunch while they're trying to take a pic of it? Yes. Do I want to photobomb the selfies they're taking at the gym? Heck yes. Do I think that they deserve the venom that's hissed at them online? Absolutely not. They've built companies out of nothing. Colour me impressed.

Back to Rachel. She's special. She's beautiful, caring, and incredibly talented. At the time I write this, she's only twenty-seven but has created a million-dollar blog and a million-dollar clothing brand, all while raising two children under the age of six. (Oh, and yes, she is very young to have two children. The Mormons pop them out young here in Utah.)

Originally, when Rach suggested going into business together, I had no interest. I didn't have a business partner, and I didn't think I ever wanted one, as I'm very set in my ways when it comes to business. However, I saw the benefit in working together. Rachel was one of the biggest bloggers, and her readers bought what she recommended. In the blogging world, conversion is very important. If your links and traffic don't convert to sales, then your follower count doesn't mean shit. But her readership was very engaged, and I thought the collection would do well.

So, after some thought, we formed a partnership. She wanted the collection to be ready in three months. Under even the best of circumstances, creating something like that would take at least six to nine months. But I said, "We'll try to create a miracle," and we did. We worked every hour that God sent. We hauled ass.

We were together every day for most hours of the day. If we couldn't meet in person, we worked on FaceTime. The collection was very pink. Rach is obsessed with pink, as highlighted by her blog, *Pink Peonies*. She wanted whimsical, flowy, and structured occasion wear. She described; I drew. By the end of the week, we had a beautiful collection in the works. Once I designed it, I went to China to start sampling, and production began within a couple of weeks.

We created a brand of premium clothing, which was something I'd never done before. We were both apprehensive—I wasn't sure we could sell at the above-$200 price point, and she didn't know how much we could sell. But we forged ahead.

She had the idea in January. We launched in April.

We sold over one thousand pieces within just one day. Holy shit, Rach had selling power like I'd never seen before.

That was the moment when I realized, with the success of all my brands, I could probably retire within the next few years. I wasn't making a fortune, but I was making enough to be able to provide a comfortable life for my husband and future kids, while maybe taking consultant work on the side. What's more, I realized that I *should* probably retire within the next few years. Mostly because trying to manage the pressure of keeping these brands afloat was going to give me a heart attack.

When I first met Rachel, I hated pink with a passion. But now I've grown to love it. She showed me the (pink) light. We knew our audience and we catered to them—a classic, feminine brand, full of dresses and skirts that were appropriate for our customers. We did a lot of fit-and-flare dresses. In America, people will purchase a fit-and-flare dress over a shift dress any day. I don't know what the fascination is to wear something so form-fitting up top and more voluminous down below, but the masses seem to love it out here. From what I've found running these apparel brands, Americans like to show off their waists and try to hide their hips, while European women don't care as much about highlighting their curves. In Europe, they'll go for a shift dress. The focus there is more on showing off their style, their fashion sense, and their ability to play with proportion, structure, and dimension.

I don't know where this American desire to show off the waist and hide the hips comes from—is it pressure from the media? Is the '50s housewife look the eternal ideal in US culture? I don't know what the psychology is behind it, but I am always amazed by how much American women gravitate toward it. My personal opinion is that while

I love a fit-and-flare, which can be very flattering and whimsical, I hate the idea that women are wearing it to hide the lower half of their curves, or using this silhouette to accommodate men's ideas of femininity and beauty.

I think a shift dress is super cool and sexy without having to high-light any part of the body. Plus, I think it really shows off creativity and style, as opposed to just showing off the female form.

But anyway, back to Rachel. We agreed to be partners for five years. Our collection was a massive success, but after a year, it became clear to me that having another business was killing me. I had moved to Utah permanently and had so much on my plate at the time. It had been so ambitious of me to think I could run three companies and still have a life and be happy.

I thought I could handle three businesses, especially since the third was an extension of what I was already doing. But having a business partner added a level of stress that I never expected. With my own busi-ness, I got to make all the decisions. But with a partner, that was no longer the case. Rachel had a million-dollar blog and an aesthetic to uphold. The details were very important to her, and I understood that. But it meant that all my decisions had to meet with her approval, and if they didn't, I would do all I could until she was happy. I realized that I had to start selling the businesses and find a way out. Rachel and I had become close friends, and I told her I was going to leave the company.

The truth is, I was starting to feel depressed, which I had never felt before. I had been blue, but this was different. I felt like my life revolved around work only. I didn't want to get out of bed. I was even miserable with my husband, which was a clear indication that something was terribly wrong. He's always able to cheer me up and bring me so much joy.

Let me say this: My depression occurred in the winter, and Utah is really bleak in January. It's cold and it's grey and it's overcast. That really compounded the issue.

Yet within a few months of juggling three businesses, I started to feel like I couldn't see a way out of it. My depression worsened, and I began to feel suicidal. Every day on my drive to or from work, I would start to fantasize about driving into oncoming traffic. I cried in my car every day, thinking I just wanted to take the easy way out.

I felt like I was drowning. I didn't want to leave a financial burden for me and for Rob. I didn't want to fail, and I didn't want to be a failure in his eyes. I thought, *If I can't turn this around, I'm going to have a heart attack.* I also wondered, *If this fails, what will I do with the rest of my life? This is all I know how to do.*

For a month, all I wanted was to end it.

Every day, Rob asked me how I was doing, and I told him I was fine. But then I'd cry really hard, which was very out of character for me. He struggled with it. He saw me cry every day, and he cried with me, too. He would say, "You don't have to do any of this. You can quit, and it will be fine." He knew that I was feeling really suicidal, and he wanted to help me out of it. On one of the worst days, I was making the fifteen-minute drive home in my Subaru Outback, when I called him from the car, saying, "I want to drive off this bridge, and I need you to talk me out of it." And he did. He was at work, and he stopped what he was doing to talk to me. I pulled over on the side of the road, and he calmed me down.

I love that boy.

When we were back home, he said, "Just walk away."

And I said, "I love you, but that's not how life works. I've got employees. I'm responsible for people's lives. I can't just walk away."

I felt like everything—including my dignity and respect—was on the line. I had gone through so many years of trying to prove myself. We had successful people in my family, but they were always middle-of-the-road successful. I love my family, but we weren't go-getters as much as we could have been. I didn't want my family to think, *He moved to America to achieve the American dream, and within a few years, he quit when it got tough.*

I felt so much self-imposed pressure to prove myself and to prove that I wasn't a failure. I had become the laughingstock of my family because I'd quit every job I ever had. But that was different.

I was also afraid to quit because I knew I didn't want to stay at home every day, because I would become even more depressed and suicidal with no purpose.

Yet I would literally kill myself if I continued at that stress level.

So I made a plan, very quickly, to sell the businesses and retire. I didn't have tens of millions of dollars, but if I sold the businesses, there was enough to be able to take care of my husband and our future children. And I planned to do consultant work in the future, so I would still have an income.

I didn't want to hurt Rachel, as we had become really close, so I talked to her husband first to see if he wanted to become part of the business. I asked him, "If I step out, could you fill my shoes?" He could take on my business role, and a technical designer could handle the design. He had wanted to be a part of the business from the start, so he was super excited.

Once I knew the business could survive, it was just about the emotional component. It was time to speak to Rachel. I told her that I needed to make a change and to focus on my real life. I wanted to have children. I wanted to pour my love into my family. I said, "Look. I love you, and I don't want you to think this is a personal thing. I'm not leaving the business because I'm not happy with you. I'm drowning, and I need to focus on myself and my family."

She wasn't angry, but she was really upset. She cried and asked if we could hire more help. She was willing to do whatever it took to keep me. We had built an amazing business and had a great relationship, but I told her that there was nothing we could do to change my mind. I had to choose family.

At the time, I wasn't willing to tell her that the pressure made me feel suicidal. I'm usually an open book about many things, but when it came to something so emotionally vulnerable, not even my good friends knew. Looking back, I think, that was nothing to be ashamed of. So many of us go through periods where we feel like we're drowning and we can't see the forest for the trees. But I wasn't willing to share it. Up until this point, I've never told her. I didn't want her to feel any added guilt that the stress from the business was causing me so much anxiety.

A couple of weeks after I announced I was leaving, I got a call about this job for Netflix.

When Rachel caught wind of the news, she thought I was leaving the company for this job, and she was incredibly hurt. I tried to explain that yes, the timing seemed very suspicious, but it was just a coincidence and a very fortuitous opportunity. I wanted to cut back, and instead, I took on one of the busiest jobs I've had in my life. But it gave me a whole new career path. It was too good to pass up. She felt that I'd lied to her, even when I did my best to explain to her that it wasn't the case.

It was hard for our relationship, but I was able to show her that I wasn't actually necessary anymore, as the business was running perfectly with the team we'd hired and that she and her husband could do it on their own. I was right about that, of course. Rachel Parcell Inc. is more successful than ever, and she and I are still friends to this day.

Selling those businesses was the best thing I ever did. I hired a broker to help with the process, and he found buyers for all the brands within a year or so. All were sold to private buyers in the apparel industry. I'd like to believe that I'm great at designing and creating a brand. But when it comes to worrying about money and production, I'm a fucking nightmare. The best advice I could ever give anyone is don't go into mass production unless you handle extreme amounts of pressure really well, because it's so, so stressful. If you can avoid it, do, unless you have millions of dollars backing it, because if something goes wrong, it will cost a fortune.

My other advice for those looking to go into business is as follows: Don't go into business thinking, *I'm going to be rich!* Don't go into business for money. Business ownership is the hardest thing. It's so not the easy ride you might think it is. You don't get to go on vacation, you don't get to chill by the pool, and if you do, you're going to get bogged down by emails and phone calls, which negates any pleasure you enjoyed while away. There's no such thing as a stress-free business. Getting rich doesn't just happen for a business owner. It's the possible payoff after many, many years of years of living a life that most people aren't willing to.

Make sure you learn everything you can and do every job you can within the field you're interested in. Don't go into a business you don't know anything about thinking you can hire people who do know. There's no reason to hire employees (or even a single employee) until you are making real money, if you know your business well.

Borrow as little money as physically possible. I was raised in a culture where finance and credit were not only frowned upon but actually forbidden. I started my business without credit, which is how I could sell it so profitably; it was all mine. (I took financing for a month, to do mass production, and I won't go into that because it's waaaaay too boring, but it wasn't regular interest-based financing.) If you do things with bank money or other borrowed money, the pressure is unbearable. You also start thinking you can spend all that money. I would never want to be a slave to debt.

Don't think you can get a salary within the first couple of years. Get another job or another stream of income, or don't quit your job just because you're starting a business.

Don't ever ask an employee to do something you wouldn't be willing to do yourself. Did I clean the office myself? Yes, I sure did. Your employees aren't your servants; they're your employees. Treat them well, and they'll work hard for you because they respect you. Don't be that fuckwit boss who makes the employees' lives hell. There's nothing strong and powerful about that. If you do that, you're just a tool.

Negativity in the office spreads like wildfire. If you see it, get rid of it. Don't be afraid to drop somebody if it seems like they'll spread negativity throughout your team. That team is precious and will encourage your company's success. You can't risk that by keeping a negative Nancy.

Do not treat your employees like your friends. They don't have to follow you on social media, and you don't have to follow them. Today, my former employees are my friends, but back when they worked for me, they were not. They were employees, and I respected them as such. Be friendly and cordial and a great colleague, but that is all. There is no reason to treat employees like friends, because when it comes down to teaching or training or discipline—or even getting rid of them— you'll find it much more difficult. I love a boundary—with friends, with family, and especially with the people who work for me.

On day one of each person's employment, we would have a conversation called the "don't be a bitch talk." Here is how it goes.

THE ART OF NOT BEING A BITCH AT WORK

I know that I can be the biggest bitch at times, so these rules are coming from a real place of knowledge. When it comes to being a bitch, I am informed. As a seasoned bitch, I know the pitfalls and also how to rein it in.

- Realize you are not in competition with everybody at your workplace.
- Realize that the success of your colleagues does not mean you're at risk of not achieving your goals.
- Do not talk about your colleagues with other colleagues, because negativity spreads like wildfire.
- If you're working at one of my offices and you dare to

bitch about a colleague so you can one-up them, know wholeheartedly that the person you're bitching about will be praised, and you, the bitching person, will be fired.

- If you're bitching about people to other people, you are the problem.
- If you truly don't appreciate something that's happening with a colleague, speak to them privately, diplomatically, and air your grievances on a professional—but not a personal—basis.

I love women, and I'm surrounded by them. In fact, most of the people in my life are women. Women are the people that have molded who I am. However, almost every woman I know has talked about equality in the workplace, about women supporting women, and about women championing other women. But I've also seen that women knock each other down and say mean things about other women more than I've ever seen from my male counterparts.

Women: Stop knocking each other down, and let's start building each other up. Men are already there to stomp on you; the last thing we need is for women to join in on the act.

PSA: LITTLE BLACK SOMETHING

I feel jealous that women have so many different options. You can wear jeans, dresses, skirts . . . if you have a whole box of crayons, why would you choose only two colours?

Drag isn't for me, personally. I think it's wonderful for people who want to do it, and I love a good drag show. It's just not my bag to dress in drag. Still, I have worn many a dress in my lifetime. Let me explain.

For the first couple of years at Kingdom & State, my very first business, I had no money for fit models, but I myself was a women's wear size medium. I knew where a dress should fall to be appropriate for a woman, and so I was the fit model for every dress, skirt, and swimsuit for the first few years in business. I would either gain or lose weight to make sure my waist and hips were the correct measurement for a size-medium woman. No joke. I would obsess over it for the run-up to sampling season and managed to get into shape each time. (See, I really did do the most to make the business work. You have to do some crazy shit if you really want to make your dreams come to life.)

A dress is an appropriate choice for any occasion and can look just as cool and sexy as jeans or a skirt. People say women shouldn't have to wear dresses, and I completely agree with that. But I do think it looks great for almost every situation, if a dress is something you gravitate toward.

For the workplace, wear what's appropriate for your style; just don't make it overly sexual. The office isn't the place to make bold, sexy fashion statements. I'm not trying to dim your shine, boo, but people at your corporate office don't need all your shine right now. They've got targets to reach.

I like the wisdom that every woman should have a little black dress that works for every occasion. But the idea that it has to be a dress is an old-fashioned notion. Maybe it's a pair of great-fitting black pants and a black top you can wear to a fancy occasion with your footwear. The idea is to have a little black something, where you know you can put it on and it won't take any effort. You can run into your closet, throw it on in two seconds, and still look stylish and chic as fuck.

JEWELLERY

One day, Rob and I were on vacation in Vegas when I received a call from Cameron, a guy I hardly knew. He was a talent manager who was connected to me through a friend of a friend. "Are you available within the next hour?" he asked. "I want you to Skype with somebody from Netflix."

Again, I barely knew this guy. And I was on vacation. Obviously, I was not doing the call. Also, I was literally about to retire and had zero interest in pursuing further work, especially in show business.

"Don't worry," he said. "It will only take an hour. They just want to talk to you, to see if you could be right for this show."

"An hour?" I replied. "I'm on vacation with my husband. I really don't think this is for me, but thanks."

Then he asked me if I had ever seen *Queer Eye for the Straight Guy.* I had seen the British version, but not the American version. Still, I had no interest in doing this call. I knew I'd never get the job, as I'd never auditioned for anything in entertainment before, and I didn't want to waste my vacation time talking to someone who would inevitably tell me I wasn't right for the role.

My husband was like, "It's only a call! Go for it!" And so, he convinced me to do it. Yes, you can all go ahead and thank Rob France right now.

I begrudgingly left the mall where I was strolling around at Caesars Palace and went back to the hotel room. I was staying at the Paris, which is an older hotel that I like because it feels a bit like Grandma's house. The rooms aren't cool and modern; they're cozy. I'm an old grandma who likes going to bed by ten, and that is what suits me. This particular room was more like WASPy Grandma's house, where even though Grandma's rich, she hasn't redecorated since the 1940s, and she hates having kids around, so there really aren't any of them rattling around the halls. Yes, please.

I dialed into the call, but as soon as the casting director saw the room—beige chintz wallpaper with blue and white flowers, and paisley carpet—he was like, "Oh no. You're going to have to go somewhere else." I thought Grandma's house was nice, but he did not agree. "This is supposed to be cool," he said. "We're recording this interview to show to Netflix. Can you speak to management? Can you tell them this call is an audition and to put you somewhere else?"

That sounded like the douchiest thing to say to the hotel manager. So before I spoke to them, I decided to try out the spa. It was cleaner and brighter and more modern, and I hoped it would work. But as soon as the call connected, fucking Enya started playing in the background. Enya!!

Enya was all, "Whoooo . . . can . . . say . . . where the rooooad goes . . ."

And the manager was like, "Nope. This won't work either."

As I left the spa, my husband saw me running around with my laptop on what was no longer a relaxing vacation. "Forget this, I'm going to tell them to leave me alone!" I told him, because I wanted to go back to the mall and enjoy the rest of my vacation. But Rob was like, "Can you calm down? Let's go speak to the manager. Just tell them you have a Netflix audition and see what they say."

Naturally, he talked to the manager, while I stood there, holding my laptop.

They agreed to give me a newly renovated conference room to use for an hour. It was white and minimal, with pops of black and red and yellow. It looked more modern and acceptable, and—apparently—cool enough for the interview. I was wearing a striped tee with my black leather moto jacket, so I guess I looked cool enough for the interview?

The call connected, and within a few minutes of speaking to the casting director, I was like, *Gosh, I like this guy!* I could tell he really liked me, too. We wound up talking for two hours. It felt super casual. He just wanted to get to know me and my opinions on life. Why did I live in Utah? How was life in America versus life in England? He asked me about my husband. Just a friendly chitchat. It was lovely, and I felt like I could actually become friends with him. That's how comfortable it was. He said this was the last day of auditions and that they had interviewed a couple thousand people for this role, but that I was his favourite.

"I don't believe you! You're just being nice," I said, because I truly thought this. He laughed and told me I had obviously never dealt with casting people before, as they aren't known for being nice. I really didn't believe him, though. I assumed he was just saying it because I was already pretty set, career-wise, and that he didn't want to hurt the feelings of someone who wasn't used to this industry. I now know better; casting directors really aren't ones for fluffing anyone up un-necessarily.

He said the next step was to turn my Skype call into a three-minute video to share with the creators of the show and that if they liked me, I would be hearing from them directly. I did not think there was any chance I would possibly get picked for this job. I used to be so uncom-fortable on camera, and I thought, *There's no way these people will want to see what I'll do in a situation where cameras are around.*

But then, a couple of days later, I heard from the creators, who wanted to schedule another call that day. Since it seemed like a long shot, I was feeling real calm and real sassy (that's my resting state), and I said whatever I wanted. Near the beginning of the call, I called one of them a cheeky bastard. He was like, "Did you really just call me a bastard?" to which I said, "Well, if you're being a bastard, I sure won't hesitate to call you that." They laughed and looked at each other like, "Well, we appreciate the honesty."

I'm not very often intimidated by people. In this case, I looked at the creators and thought, *You've got a job, I've got a job. You're success-ful, I'm successful. Why should I feel intimidated? If this goes nowhere, I'm happy with my lot in life.* When we got to the end of the call, they thought they had hung up, but there was a three-second delay. Be-fore the line officially cut off, I heard the show's creator say, "Holy fuck!" and he jumped out of his chair. I thought, *I may have done all right.*

Later on that day, I got a call from the casting guy, who told me, "You're the one! I knew it. We're pushing forward." He said the final stage was a three-day audition in Los Angeles, where I would meet forty-something other men all vying for a place in the cast.

I was still adamant this was not my job. In my heart of hearts, I didn't think this would work out. I didn't think they really liked me for the job—I thought they were just being kind and wanted to make sure it seemed like they were diversifying with a token brown immi-grant. So again, I told them I couldn't do it. I said I couldn't take three days out of my life. After all, I was in the process of selling my final business, and I had a lot going on. Selling a business is so stressful. It's like tax season times ten or like applying for a mortgage for a house that you know is out of your damn price range. There was so much paperwork involved, and the thought of taking a quick sunny break to LA to try to get a job I was determined I would never actually get just seemed so stupid. But once again, Rob convinced me I should go. He reminded me that I had recently said I wanted to make more gay friends. My only gay man friend at the time was . . . my husband, as I worked every hour that God sent, and I lived in Salt Lake, where mak-ing gay friends wasn't the easiest. He made a fair point that in a room full of forty-two gay men, I could probably make friends with some of them. So that was what I set out to do. I was going to go take advantage of a huge audition and return home knowing I now had some new gay mates.

We were told the first night of auditions would be a cocktail party, so we could "get to know each other and make friends."

It was a chemistry test.

This made me nervous. I still didn't feel nervous about the show, mind you, but I hadn't been out to a bar or club in about ten years, and I knew everyone would be clamoring for attention. My resting state is that I'm a dweeb. I don't drink, I don't dance, and no one would ever accuse me of being cool. I get nervous in crowds and just want to skulk off into a corner until I can slip away without anyone noticing I'm gone.

I arrived at the cocktail party to find what looked like a mosh pit— everyone had crowded around the bar, while the rest of the room remained empty, save for the high cocktail tables they had placed in the center. I wanted nothing to do with that mosh pit situation, as I had no idea how I'd even begin to infiltrate, so I thought, *I'm going to station myself at one of these tables. If people want to talk to me, hopefully they'll come over and chat one-on-one.*

Weirdly, people kept coming over until there was a gaggle of gays with me, all chatting and having a laugh. I'm quite sociable one-on-one and can speak to people for hours on end, as long as I don't feel pressure to be cool or land a TV job. So this setup was especially great, because I wasn't trying to get the job; I was just trying to make a friend. And already I had found a couple of people I thought I could be friends with, and still am friends with, to this day!

One of them was Karamo. I remember thinking, *Gosh, you're attractive.* He makes such intense eye contact, where he looks you deep in the eye as he's shaking your hand, and it's like everything else disappears. That night, I thought it was just for me—that I was special. Since then, I've learned that little shit is just a highly skilled schmoozer, and he does that to everyone. It's a skill I wish I had.

I also noticed Bobby, who was wearing something zany—a brightly coloured suit and very thick-rimmed glasses. He was very animated and really stood out to me.

Meanwhile, everyone had been talking about how hot this guy Antoni was. I kept looking around the room like, "Who are you talking about?" When it became clear who they were talking about, I thought, *Really? That guy?* Antoni is obviously incredibly handsome, but he just really wasn't my type. He seemed like a nice guy, and I wanted him to get the job, but he had a nervous, shy energy about him and seemed way too sweet and angelic. I couldn't picture us being friends, as I usually gravitate to folks who are a lot more outgoing than I am.

It's so ironic that was my first impression of him, because of course, now he is my favourite person on the planet (besides my husband), and I love him more than life itself. He is my brother for life, who is definitely not as sweet and innocent as he seemed at that first encounter.

Then there was Jonathan.

Cameron, the manager who had first called me in Vegas, was actually Jonathan's former manager, and all along he kept telling me, "Look for Jonathan Van Ness—you're going to love him!"

Well, out of the forty-two people at the cocktail party, he was the forty-second one I spoke to, at the very end of the evening. And when I met Jonathan, I thought, *There is no way I'm ever going to see this guy again.* He came up to me and started talking very loudly about his intimate life. I wasn't used to a person I'd just met speaking so frankly with me about his sexual escapades. I was like, "There is no way I could ever work with this person, and there is no way I could ever be friends with him." I thought he was a shoo-in for the show, of course, and that he really had something special. But he had so much personality; I didn't think we would get along. A little over a month later, he, too, became one of my favourite people. Apparently, my initial instincts are very, very wrong.

For the second round of the callback, everyone played a game of casting speed dating. There were four tables, and at each table there were three auditioners and one producer. They called us in alphabetical order, and since my name starts with *T*, I got to hear some of the questions being asked of the guys who went ahead of me.

Each table had a fishbowl in the center, filled with slips of paper bearing topical questions. When it was my turn, one of the producers asked me if I'd like to take a question from the bowl, and I said no. I said, "I've heard the kind of questions that are in this bowl, and I have no desire to talk about the last time I flew a kite or what kind of dog I had. I want to ask *you* questions and talk about things that are more interesting." They were shocked. I went on, "I'm British. I don't do small talk. I like to chat about real things. I heard you recently got divorced; tell me about it. Do you have kids? What was the reason for the divorce? I'd love to hear more about that."

They were like, "What? You're asking *us* the questions?"

When our time was up, they still wanted to get to know me more, and I said, "That's why I don't do fishbowl questions."

On the second day of auditions, we were told to bring a personal item. It was supposed to be something that meant a lot, something we could talk about. The whole thing would be filmed.

I was actually in Vegas again when I got the call to head to LA for this live audition, so I wasn't able to bring anything from home that was personal to me. When it was my turn, I said I didn't bring anything. But I told the producers the only thing I carry with me is my wedding ring. I explained how my marriage and my husband have shaped my life. I told them how everything I am and everything I will ever be is because of our partnership and what the ring signifies. I went on about how Rob is the most wonderful man in the world, how he is the reason I live in America, how he is the reason I'm going to retire and have children, and how he is the reason everything I'd ever dreamed about was made possible. "There was no reason to bring any other personal belonging with me," I told them. "I have all I need right here in this wedding ring."

At the end of my speech, a few of the producers were crying. Again, I thought, *I may have done all right.*

The next day, I was called back in. The producers had Karamo, Bobby, and me sit in a room and answer questions while sitting in front of a bunch of cameras and producers. They kept rotating different auditionees in and out, but I remained. They also kept rotating in JVN and Ant. That was the day I fell in love with them both, along with Karamo and Bobby. We learned so much about each other within those few hours and were having such a laugh. It went on this way for eight hours. I was one of the only people who sat in that room the entire time. They either really liked what I was doing, or I wasn't doing enough and they wanted to give me a chance to stop screwing it up. Either way, I was grateful.

I wasn't nervous, even with the cameras pointing at me. I just pretended they weren't there. I don't know where that ability came from. I just chatted with the auditionees and had fun. I didn't try too hard. I was just myself. The same Tan France you see on the show.

At one point, there were five people in the room, and the producers told us there were only five other people in the holding room. It was down to ten. That was the first time I thought, *Holy fuck, I might get this job.*

The very last stage of the callback was to do a mini discovery scene. We'd act like we were on the show—we'd ambush someone's house (just like the opening part of a real episode), I'd go into the closet and take a look and tell them what I didn't like about it and what we'd need to change.

This was my first time ever being on camera alone, and I sucked ass. I was so aware of the fact that I was being filmed. I also kept talking directly to the camera, like it was an audience. They were all, "Stop talking to the camera!" But I couldn't stop. They also told me to Americanize what I was doing, and I got really upset. I was like, "I am a Brit. This is how I do things. I can't be more American." And quite frankly, I had no desire to be. I liked not being over-animated.

I think they wanted me to speak loudly, use my body a lot more, and act a little cheesy, but that's definitely not my personality. That kinda thing makes me feel embarrassed for others when I see them doing it. There's no way I could do that myself. I wanted to remain true to myself and show them how I would actually work the scene if I were on the show, not ham it up for the audition and then not be able to re-create that for the actual job.

Then, after that part of the audition, we were all sent home. In the car on my way to the airport, I remember thinking, *Gosh, I sucked at that. There is no way I'm going to get this job.* But I had convinced myself that I hadn't really wanted it anyway. And so, I went back to Utah. Did I really want the job? Heck yeah, of course I did. I just didn't *want* to want it, as I honestly didn't think there was a hope in heaven of me getting it. So, I blocked out the desire for it. Apparently, I'm quite the doomsday-er.

At this point, however, I had gotten what I'd set out for, which was gay friends. Bobby, Karamo, Jonathan, Antoni, and I had created a group text called "Fab 5." Mind you, we hadn't been chosen at this point, but we really liked each other and wanted to stay in touch. I knew that even if I didn't get it, I wanted to stay in touch with these boys and hang out again. They were wicked.

I left LA on a Sunday. On Friday, five days later, I got a call from my casting director who said they wouldn't have an answer until Monday or Tuesday at the earliest. Up until that point, it was such a freakin' rough five days. I could hardly sleep. Even though I thought I knew the outcome, I would replay the whole audition in my mind and toy with the hope that maybe I would get it and how much that would change the course of my life. Then, with the next breath, I'd remind myself of why it was never going to happen, and they would never be crazy enough to hire a complete novice.

An hour later, I got a call from a California number. I thought, *Oh, shit, they're calling me to tell me I didn't get the job. Monday is when they're telling the people who got it.*

I answered the phone, and before they could even speak, I said, "I'm so sorry. I tried really hard, and I know you were rooting for me.

But I was retiring anyway, and so it's really fine! I'm so sorry I let you down."

They said, "I'm so sorry to have to tell you this, but we'll need you to come out of retirement."

I said, "*No way!* Give it to the other guy! He wants it so badly. I'm going to ruin the show!"

And they laughed and replied, "We know how to cast a show. You're going to be amazing."

And that was that. I got it.

We hung up, and I screamed into my pillow. Then I instantly got up, grabbed my keys, and headed to the hospital where Rob works to tell him the news. The whole ten-minute drive there felt like I was watching a movie of someone else's life. I just kept screaming, "Holy shit!" in my car. I truly couldn't believe that they'd chosen me. I had gotten it. I had to keep telling myself that this was real. I was going to be on a show. Even though I knew it was true, part of my brain was trying to convince me that it was all a dream. It was the weirdest feeling.

When I got to the hospital and parked, the walk to Rob's office was intense. I was practically giddy with excitement. I didn't run (South Asian guys can't run in hospitals, either), but I was desperate to get there and tell him. When I arrived, he was sitting at his desk with people milling around it. As soon as he saw me approach, he knew instantly from my smile that it was good news. He whisper-screamed, and I whisper-screamed back. We hugged so hard for what felt like minutes. I'll never forget how proud he made me feel.

The casting directors let me know the cast was Bobby, Karamo, Jonathan, and me. They hadn't yet decided on the food guy and were considering someone else. But of course, we all wanted it to be Antoni.

I didn't hesitate to share this opinion with the casting directors. I called them and was like, "I love Antoni. It *has* to be Antoni." I sent them impassioned messages telling them why this was so. They were like, "Bish, know your place. You don't get to decide." But the other boys and I were so pushy about Antoni being the one that they brought him back out for a second audition. And lo and behold, Antoni got the job, because on that second audition, he showed just how perfect he was for the show.

We were told that filming would start in four weeks and we were moving to Atlanta for the summer. When we got to Atlanta to start filming, shit really got real. It was a big crew, there were a lot of cameras around, and everyone was talking about how huge this show would be. Every day for three weeks, I was in a panic. I couldn't stop thinking, *I'm doing the worst job* ever. *There's no way I'm good at this, and I will never feel comfortable enough around a camera to be myself and, more importantly, to be happy.*

It really hit when we wrapped on Cory the cop's episode. That had been shot as the second episode, so I had two weeks under my belt at that point. I hadn't gotten any real feedback, so all I had were my own opinions on my performance, and because I'm always my own worst critic, I'd convinced myself that I sucked on camera. I worried I was too quiet and not fun enough for the rest of the cast. I felt like I was bringing them down. I also didn't understand so much of the terminology, and I felt stupid asking, so I didn't. This meant I was always making technical mistakes, like not knowing when I wasn't in shot or when the camera couldn't see my face properly. All of this to say, *I* was the reason I was struggling so much. I didn't do all I could to learn the things I didn't know, and I was making set life harder for myself.

Late one night, I couldn't take it anymore. I went to the apartment of the show's creator, David, and knocked on his door. He could immediately tell something was wrong. I sat on his couch and cried and cried. "I'm not doing well, I can't do this job, I'm ruining the show," I told him. "I want out of my contract. I know you guys are going to fire me, so I'll go now and won't take any legal action if you don't take any legal action against me." That was how convinced I was that I wasn't doing well on the show and that I would never make it in this industry.

I had been watching the other boys on set, and I couldn't be like them. They never seemed nervous; in fact, they were the opposite. They were expressive and dramatic and American. They would wear the heroes' (clients') crazy clothes and play with toys and make jokes. All I knew how to do was be this more reserved British person.

The producers kept saying, "Energy! Energy, Tan!" I was trying to act like a showbiz person, and it just wasn't me.

I explained to the creator that I didn't fit in because I couldn't be something I'm not. I don't do slapstick. I don't do over the top—I do snarky. I'm not American. Brits don't love to be cheesy. I'm not willing or able to be someone else.

He looked at me and said, "But the best moments are when you're *you*. Please don't put this pressure on yourself." His words made me understand that I could make this experience my own. All this time, I thought they wanted to me to be a person I wasn't. It took David telling me to block out all those thoughts and just be myself that really spun it for me. They had hired me for who I truly was, not a character I wasn't willing to play.

The next day, I went into work with a completely different mentality, and the game changed. I played my role, but I was empowered to play it the way I wanted it. Completely honestly. I was much happier for it, and I think it makes for both an authentic show and an authentic Tan.

So many times, I think we do things because we don't want to cause an issue. I wish I had spoken up earlier, instead of going along with something because I thought it was what was expected of me. All I can say is speak up; ask questions. Explain your concerns. It's the first step in feeling empowered to push forward with your own agenda. There is no reason to stifle yourself! Because as a wise man once told me: the best moments are the ones where you're *you*.

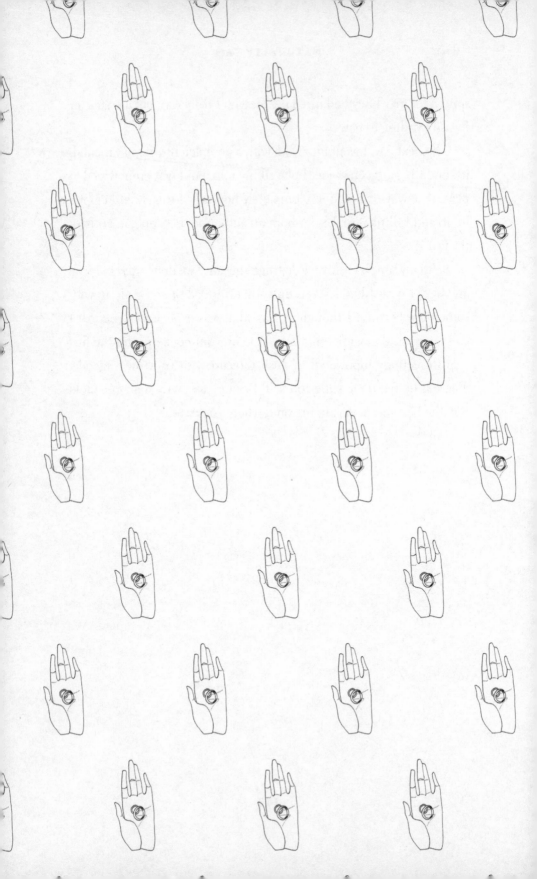

WEDDING RING

I've told you about how important my wedding ring is to me, but I'd also like to share the story behind it.

When Rob and I decided to get married, it wasn't really a conversation. There was no proposal. There was no need for a proposal. We mentioned wanting to get married only a month and a half into knowing each other, when Rob first visited me in England. At that time, of course, it would have been insane. So we left it alone until a year or so later, when it came up again. "I could marry you today," he said. "I could marry you," I said. And this time, we said, "Well, then, let's do it!" and went down to the marriage registry office.

When you get married in the UK, you have to register at least two weeks prior. In order to do this, you get all your documents together and you meet with a clerk who tries to ascertain whether it's a legitimate marriage or not. On the day we registered, Rob and I sat in an office with a sweet, bubbly lady. She walked us through basic questions, and then it came time give our parents' occupations. I said my mom had been a housewife. Then it was Rob's turn. He had to give an honest answer, and he said, "Cowboy and cowgirl." The woman enjoyed this so much! She said, "I've never gotten to write that before! Do you mind if I tell people?" It reminded me how nuts it was that this Pakistani boy from England was marrying a legitimate cowboy.

When Rob and I got married, I was living in England during the early days of Kingdom & State, and the business was struggling. We were making ends meet, but we weren't making a real profit. We were broke as a joke, but luckily men's wedding bands aren't as costly as women's diamond rings, and I knew exactly what I was looking for. I wanted my ring to be Indian gold, which is yellower and purer and softer than Western gold. I asked Rob if he minded, and he said he liked it, so we went ahead and chose our bands.

Rob was back visiting America at the time, but I told him to measure his wedding ring finger so I could have the rings made in time for the wedding. He did and shared the information. He said he was a size nine. I said, "That *cannot* be right."

He told me it was.

I said, "I've been with you for two years, and I know with absolute certainty that is not your size. Go back and check it."

"Tan, that is one hundred percent right," he said.

Against my better judgment, I told him I would try my best to accept it as true. But I knew it had to be wrong, because it sounded like it was meant for the thumb ring of a fucking giant. However, I was trying to not be the bitch from hell and not scare him off marrying me, so I agreed to the ring size he was suggesting. Also, you might remember that I love an "I told you so" moment, and I could feel one coming that was so strong that I definitely didn't want to miss it.

The salesperson rang me up, and Rob's ring was triple the price of mine. I'm standing there thinking, *I'm broke as a joke and this guy is going to take me for every penny I've got.* But Rob was absolutely adamant that it was the right size. So, if I'm marrying the man, it starts with trust . . . even when he's clearly wrong.

A few days later, our rings arrived. We decided not to try them on before we said our vows.

I distinctly remember waking up on the morning of our wedding, turning to Rob, and talking about getting married for the very first time. We were so matter-of-fact about it—we had booked the date, we decided we wanted just the two of us and a couple of witnesses—but we hadn't really discussed *marriage.* That morning, I turned to him and said, "Have we really thought about this? This is a lifetime commitment. Have we truly thought it through?"

"I feel the exact same way," he said. "We probably should have talked about this."

I knew I wanted to spend my life with him. We talked about

everything—about life, about timing, about whether we wanted to have kids. But we didn't talk about the complexities of marriage and how, if we ever wanted to get out of it, there would be a lot of legalities involved. In the end, though, I think it was just a regular case of cold feet.

Though we were really struggling financially, we purchased suits for the wedding. But when the day rolled around, Rob's suit wasn't fitting him very nicely and he wasn't feeling good about it. So I gave him my suit to wear, which fit him beautifully. I wore his suit, which I didn't really like and which didn't fit me right, either. He could see that it wasn't working, but I didn't care; I just wanted him to feel good. He was always the one who beat himself up about his appearance more than I did, and I thought, *It's our wedding day. I want him to feel great.* And he looked fantastic.

We didn't get many pictures taken that day. I didn't want them, as I knew no matter what, I would remember it forever. But there is one photo of us that was taken by a friend, and every time I see it, I'm like, *You moron, you should have just worn your own suit.* At the time, it felt very romantic, but the photo lives on.

Once we were in our wedding suits, we traveled on the tube along with our friends who served as witnesses, Naznin and Nasrin (sisters), and Nasrin's fiancé, John. As we walked into Islington Town Hall, we were both weirdly nervous but excited. We walked up and gave our information and then sat for twenty minutes, waiting for our names to be called. I paced a bit.

Finally, we heard our names and went to the room for the ceremony. It wasn't at all what I expected. It was tiny and very gaudy, with a floral carpet and chintzy wallpaper. I'm sure it cost a lot, but it looked like Grandma decorated it. It had enough chairs lined up for fifty people, but we only had our three witnesses.

Rob and I went to the front of the room and stood next to this dude, as you would at any wedding. We giggled a lot through the ceremony, partially because we were nervous and partially because we giggle a lot anyway.

Rob sometimes had trouble understanding English accents. During the ceremony, one of the lines was, "I promise to love and respect you always," and Rob said, "I promise to love and respect your ways." We all laughed so much at that one, because it sounded like he was saying he planned to respect my crazy South Asian ways.

The officiant asked if this was our version of a green card marriage, because he had never seen anyone behave this way during a ceremony. We assured him it wasn't.

Then I smiled and slipped the ring onto his finger. It looked like it was King Kong's wedding ring. I was pissed, but we were getting married, so this was Rob's lucky day. To this day, Rob counts his lucky stars that we didn't open up the package with our rings enclosed before the wedding day.

In our vows, we had changed the traditional line "I will love and obey you" to cut out the word *obey*. But as we said our vows, he forgot and added it back in.

I stood there thinking, *When I tell you a ring is too big, you will listen. Obey.*

Of course, we had to have it resized the next day.

As it turns out, Rob is a size seven, not a size nine.

Yep, I love an "I told you so" more than anything in this world. My instincts are usually good, and when I tell someone "I told you so," it's for a very good reason. If you were to ask my closest friends, "What does Tan love more than anything in this world?" they will say, "An 'I told you so'" . . . quickly followed by cake.

I'd love to be a better person, but I just like being right. And baked goods.

After the ceremony, we went to a high tea our friends had arranged as a gift for us, and then back to our apartment, where we ate wedding cake and watched TV. It was exactly as we wanted it to be. It wasn't about a wedding. It wasn't about a party. It was about us.

There was no need for the whole hoo-ha. Don't get me wrong—some proposals are very romantic, and some weddings are very nice. But I think if you have to have a big wedding to prove your love for each other, that rings alarm bells.

Now we've been married for almost ten years, and we forget our anniversary every year. We technically have two anniversaries—one when we got married in the UK, and another when we got married in the US. The month will roll around, and we'll be like, "Oh, shit, it's the month we got married." But we don't remember the day until after the fact.

The truth is, we're not the kind of people who care about anniversaries. We also don't celebrate Valentine's Day. Those types of grand gestures mean nothing to me. We're not romantic in a commercial sense, but we are in terms of our small, everyday actions. Those everyday actions add up to far more than grand gestures ever could.

I think it helps that we went into our marriage with similar expectations. I'm still very much South Asian, no matter how Western I may seem. As a traditionally minded person, divorce was never an option for me. And coming from a Mormon community, Rob also did not see divorce as an option. Of course, divorce does occur in both of our communities, but it's very rare. Even though, in marrying a man, it wasn't seen as a very "traditional" marriage, I am still a very traditional person, and I went into this thinking, *This is my only option, this is my only partner.* I knew that once I said, "I will marry you," I truly meant it, for life. That no matter what happens, we will inevitably resolve things so that we can move forward.

That's not to say everything has always been completely perfect. We've had some issues with communication. Rob comes from the sweetest, most loving family who are experts at avoiding confrontation. If there were an Olympic sport for avoidance, his family would for sure win the gold. And Rob is their star player.

When we started dating, he was able to avoid any kind of discomfort like no one I've ever met. Meanwhile, I am the complete opposite. If there is ever a problem, everyone knows that Tan is the one who starts the conversation about it, because I can't stand looming drama! But I think Rob thought I was picking on him.

Rob was raised on a ranch, and as a ranch child, you have chores. In addition to going to school, you have to tend the cows, milk the cows, herd the cows . . . (Yes, I never thought this was something I would have to consider at any point in my life.) So as an adult, he doesn't love chores. He doesn't relish being told what to do. So if I would say, "While I'm at work, you've got a couple of days off; could you go to the grocery store and get *x*, *y*, *z*?" He would get really sulky and wouldn't say anything about it until I had to shake him and say, "What the heck is going on?"

So early on, I encouraged him to tell me immediately whatever he was thinking.

Mind you, I'm not saying I'm an angel. I can be very abrasive, and sometimes the way I speak isn't polite. But something that is important to us, even eleven years on, is to use our *pleases* and *thank yous*. We're very sweet and kind to one another, to the point where friends are sometimes shocked by it. We'll always open the door and fight over who goes first. We are very respectful to each other, because that's how I see a happy relationship working.

I don't appreciate when partners belittle each other in front of other people, or where they expect the other person to do something without a *please* or a *thank you*. The same goes for arguments—there is no need to ever have an argument in public. No matter what happens in public, even if it's something upsetting, there is no way on God's earth Rob would hear about it at the event or in front of our friends. To belittle your partner in front of anybody is a horrible thing to do.

Until I met Rob, I thought, *Relationships are miserable. Relationships are hard. But there are things about relationships that make them worth it.* Now, I see that I was completely fucking wrong. You should expect to be happy every day. Anyone who says marriage is hard might need to see someone. My marriage is the easiest thing in my life. Other things are hard, and the thing that makes everything easier is my marriage. That's not to say that a marriage is without challenges, but *hard* should not be your general state.

It's a sorry state of affairs when I see someone around me struggling. Like when someone says they want to escape their partner—like physically escape. When a person tells me they're going on vacation with their girl or guy friends because they need a weekend off from their marriage or that they're so happy to get time apart, I think, *What the fuck is going on in your house?*

If ever we run into a conflict, because divorce isn't an option for us, I always know we can find a compromise and that it will be solved. Have we settled? One hundred percent not. The love we had initially is something we always remember and find our way back to. Maybe once a year, we'll have a big argument that blows up and lasts a few days, but we always find a way to resolve it.

I think part of the reason our marriage works is because we managed to come up with a life plan before we actually got married. All those Skype calls, when we were long distance and that was our main form of interaction, really did help. We discussed everything beforehand, how many children we would want, where we would live, the state of our finances and how we would manage them. Of course we're not the same people now that we were eleven years ago, but the way we live and our daily lives are the same.

The important thing is that we were on the same page about all of it. If you're having these conversations with someone and they're not on the same page as you, it may be a red flag. You have to keep having conversations to see if maybe you can get there.

Do I think I'm just lucky? No. I knew what I was looking for. I wanted somebody who wasn't a drinker. I wanted someone who had a job and a career, but also passions and ambitions. I liked that Rob was an artist. We complemented each other. I chose wisely. I didn't have to cajole him into being these things. We compromised on some things; we made verbal agreements. Was it hard work before marriage? Some of it was. It was having the courage to be very open and honest with each other so we could iron out the kinks. It wasn't luck; it was work. And it was worth it.

PSA: A WORD ON ACCESSORIES

There's that saying from Coco Chanel, "Before you leave the house, look in the mirror and take one thing off." If you've regularly been told you're overdoing it, then maybe this is good advice for you. You can't wear statement things all the time, or people will tell you that you're starting to look like a complete twat. Styling shouldn't be as difficult for us all at this point. I think we should be more evolved by now. We have so much access to styling options that we shouldn't necessarily have to take one thing off before leaving the house, as we would have already chosen a look based on inspo we found on social media, no?

My advice is this: accessorize whenever possible. It can be as simple as adding a watch or a pair of earrings, a necklace or a statement shoe. Anyone can put on a pair of jeans and a T-shirt, but that one added step of adding a piece of jewellery or bold accessory elevates it and makes your look so much more than a generic, basic look.

Find a signature accessory that works for you. You can change it every so often. You don't have to change up your wardrobe completely, but you can make it feel new by changing up your accessories.

On jewellery:

When it comes to outfits, I like to keep them quite simple. Off the show, you'll usually find me in a black or white tee, a pair of jeans, sneakers, and a load of rings.

I wear a lot of jewellery. Of course, I wear my wedding band every day, but I like to wear a lot of rings. I'll often wear at least five other rings in addition to my wedding band. It's gaudy in a way that I love and packs a punch in the bling department. Perfect.

I don't love a lot of gaudy in any other aspect of wardrobe or fashion, but when it comes to jewellery, I kind of like when it's tacky every now and then. Antoni has taken to calling me "Persian Prince" whenever I've got my jewellery on. I think it shows people I've considered my look. Don't be afraid to accessorize.

Personally, I like to wear gold jewellery—never silver. In fact, I've never, ever worn anything silver (other than a belt buckle). To me, silver feels a little hippie dippy, especially when teamed with turquoise. It definitely works on some people! I'm just not one of those people. Gold suits my brown skin beautifully, so it's here to stay.

On belts:

Someone on the show once asked why I don't wear belts. The answer is I don't wear one unless it's a statement belt. I'd rather someone wear a pair of pants that fit properly than to wear a belt. To me, belts are for fashion, never for function. Just wear the right size pants, for goodness' sake.

A belt can sometimes age a guy. If someone is wearing a boring, let's say, "office style" belt, it's dull and is going to make you look like a grown-up. Who wants to look like a grown-up? I also don't love a belt with a suit, because I think it can make it look fussy. It can also verge into "daddy" real quick.

One of my biggest pet peeves in life is an ill-fitting suit worn with a belt. It looks like you're wearing your granddad's suit. It's not cool or sophisticated, and you're definitely not planning anything sexual after this. No one wants to sleep with the ill-fitting suit guy. You're either going to work or church, and there is no chance of fun afterward. If a woman or man sees a guy wearing that ill-fitting suit and they *still* want to get some naughtiness on, well, more power to them, but this dude's probably going to close his eyes during the act and then cry afterward. Women everywhere—be warned.

In conclusion, men: wear a suit that fits and drop the functional belt.

On matching your shoes to your bag:
I recently watched a dating show where some guy had picked an outfit for this young woman. She was all excited that he clearly had style because he picked a bag and shoes that matched. I sat there on the couch with my husband screaming at the TV, "Run! Run! He thinks you're going to be his little lady!" In my opinion, it's so dated to have your shoes and your handbag match. Just get a handbag you like and don't worry about it matching with your shoes.

On finding inspiration from other cultures:

I've taken to wearing mehndi (henna body art) on the backs of my hands for events like the premiere of *Queer Eye*. I like the way it looks and also that it pays homage to my culture. You definitely don't want to co-opt another culture, especially in this current climate, but you can take references and inspiration from other cultures. Should you wear a burka if you're not Muslim? Absolutely not. But there is a way to take inspiration from other cultures, whether through your jewellery, or certain fabrics or colours or prints, without it becoming an ill-advised political statement.

But I swear, if there is one thing I hate, it's Aztec-print leggings. They've been around for so long now, and I need them to die. The kind of person who wears Aztec fucking leggings went to a yoga class eight years ago, and now they wear them every Sunday for brunch thinking maybe they'll go back to the yoga class, but they never do. They've maybe visited India once. *I've found my people!* they think. You haven't found your people; you've found *my* people. Take those fucking leggings off.

On white shoes:

As a general rule of thumb, I encourage men to wear plain white sneakers because it goes with almost everything, but I don't love white, heeled boots for women. Every now and then, it comes back in style, but I still say it's a bad idea. You never want to get yourself into a situation where somebody has to ask, "How much do you charge for a handy and some over-the-pants action?"

On shoes to avoid at all costs:

Crocs. Do not wear them.

I called them the "given up on life" shoes on *Queer Eye*, and I stand by that wholeheartedly. I understand that you think they're comfortable, but if you wear them, I will point and laugh, and I will continue to point and laugh until you take them off. If you're single and wearing Crocs and you're worried about being single, all you have to do is look down at your feet and wonder, *Am I the reason I'm single?* and know the answer is yes.

The same goes for any kind of jelly shoes for grown-ups.

Men, if you're not on the beach or imminently getting into a pool, there is no excuse for wearing flip-flops. Get a pair of slides. I don't care how many times somebody's told you that you have feet good enough to be a foot model. You don't. If you got a pedicure, so be it; I'm sure the person at the salon is very grateful you came in. Still, I don't want to look at your feet in flip-flops, and no one else does, either.

On sandals for men:

I can make my peace with sandals, to a certain extent. Before I moved to America, I was like, "What the hell is wrong with you?" about any guy wearing sandals. Especially when traveling and representing your country outside the US. But now I do see the reasoning behind sandals, and I think they're at least more acceptable than flip-flops. But do understand that they are only acceptable when worn casually and paired with an appropriate outfit. However, sandals do not say, "I've made an effort." They say, "I'm chillin' and maybe down for a second round of drinks."

SUPERMARKET

There are some major cultural differences between the US and the UK, and I didn't want to hide them, especially on the show. The other boys can be more emotional, more vulnerable, while I'm not a big crier. Americans are very aware and in tune with their emotions. It seems that their emotions are always closer to the surface, and they express them freely.

In my experience, Americans can be very passive-aggressive. In England, you're raised to be more aggressive and more direct. I think in the UK we deal with our emotions much differently at a much earlier age.

To this day, every time I travel, the first thing I do on the first day I get back to Salt Lake is to go to the supermarket. After ten years, it hasn't lost its appeal.

Grocery stores in other countries are normal. They have normal produce and maybe ten kinds of cereal. In the aisle where the cereal is, there will be maybe seventy-five other things. In America, there is *one cereal aisle*. The cereal aisle contains *only* cereal. There is a problem here.

I see these people who go on bus tours of America, and I think the first stop should be the grocery store. I used to take pictures of the produce section and send it to my family. I couldn't get over how weird it was. Everything was so perfect. Everything was so shiny.

Ever since the show blew up, my husband doesn't like to go to the grocery store together. People will stop and ask to take photos, and it takes forever to get any actual shopping done. But he won't take that away from me. I still need to wander up and down the aisles, thinking, *Ahhhhh, I've moved to America and I've got all the cereal options available to me.*

When I first moved here, I didn't understand the appeal of a car that can fit seventy-five people. The number of massive SUVs here blew my mind. As I'm saying this, I am actually looking at purchasing an SUV. I am now an American, and I want a big car, too.

Another thing I can't get over is the credit situation. Everyone here has a brand-new car! If your car is a few years old, people will shame you. On the whole, if you've got money in America, you buy stuff, but if you don't have money in America, you also buy stuff. If you want the dream, you've got the dream. That is terrifying.

As a foreigner, that feels like some fucked-up shit to me. Back home, if you've got a car that's five to ten years old, that's seen as a relatively new car, and you've done well.

While we're on the topic of finances, the only thing I really struggled with when moving to the US was tax stuff. When I first came here, I didn't realize people in the United States file their own taxes. I find it so weird that everyone is trusted to do that. I once watched someone do it and they put in deductions here and deductions there. So basically, what your tax code is saying is that if you're a smart person, you can kind of game the system. I think it's strange to leave the taxes in the hands of the people. It's very complicated! And if you make any errors, they're on your ass like crazy. I figured, it must be a topic that's covered in school, since it's something everyone will have to learn! But no. You just have to figure it out.

Plus, Americans pay more in taxes than we do in the UK, where we get free health care and mostly free education.

Speaking of health care, I once had this conversation with my father-in-law, who I love very, very, very much. It was very early on, when Rob and I were dating, and he said, "As you know, you guys have to wait way longer to see a doctor, and it's never as good. It makes sense that we have to pay for it. Free health care is never a good service, and it causes people problems."

I said, "When did you last live in England?"

"Never."

"Have you ever been there?" I asked.

"No."

"So where did you learn this?"

"Fox."

Let me set the record straight. For anyone who believes this about the health care system in the UK, it is not the case. I've waited much longer to see a doctor in the US than I ever have in the UK, and the doctors in the UK are great.

Yes, some of your hospitals are prettier. But I don't think I care about a pretty hospital.

There are so many problems with your system. You wind up paying for your care and your drugs. And insurance! It doesn't make any sense. It costs a fortune, but my biggest gripe is that you have to pay a deductible. I'd never even heard the word *deductible* back home. If you're paying insurance, the whole point is that you should be covered. Why are you expected to pay $2,000 on top of what you've been paying these people for *years?*

For anyone not in America, you will be fascinated to know, before I was hired for the show, I had been looking into getting private health insurance and it would've cost me $1,000 a month, with a deductible on top of that. If you think that makes sense, then you've drunk the Kool-Aid. It's the best con, and it's perfectly legal.

People will often ask, "Is it weird to drive on the other side of the road?"

And I'll tell them, "I'm not just driving on the other side of the road, I'm also sitting on the other side of the car!" It's only confusing when I'm just arriving in or just coming back from the UK. It always takes a day or two to acclimate.

What's even weirder to me are American cars. When I first drove here, I felt like I was driving a go-kart because I wasn't used to driving automatic. In the UK, we drive stick and have three gears, but here in the US, you only have two. It makes me wonder why we needed all these gears in the first place.

I am also confused by brunch. "Do you want to go to brunch?" an American will ask. So you say, "What time?" and they reply, "2:00 p.m."

That is lunch. That is literally lunch. Breakfast and lunch have been mashed together as a word, because it happened between breakfast and lunch. But 3:00 p.m. is no longer time for breakfast. Put your pancakes away.

When it comes to food, the way Rob and I eat is very different. When we first started dating, I remember being very surprised by it, but now it's something I observe in almost everyone here. Americans lean really far forward and, using just their right hand, shovel their food in with a fork. I remember telling Rob it's like watching a pig at a trough. In England, we hold our fork in our left hand and our knife with our right. You take small bites, never trying to fit a lot in your mouth, and it's more graceful.

I always think it's interesting eating at an Indian restaurant—in either country—because none of the people eating there are ever Indian. When I'm eating Indian food, I always eat it the traditional way, as we would in India, which is with my hands. But it's always amazing to see the looks of absolute shock on people's faces. Now Rob eats Indian food with his hands, too, and we shock everyone together.

The dating culture in the US is also something I find interesting. When it comes to dating, I think in Europe we're more comfortable saying, "Let's go on a date," and we're more aggressive in pursuing people when we're interested in them.

Here, it frustrates me when friends will tell me stories of people saying, "Wanna hang out?" over and over again. Is this a test drive? Are you trying to get out of an obligation? Shit or get off the pot. Let someone know you want to date them. Let someone know if you want to see them again. Let someone know if you don't want to see them again. As I say out on the road: signal your intentions.

Some of the colloquial differences in vocabulary have provided some funny moments. Rob has a friend whose husband owns a pawn shop. We don't have the word *pawn* in the UK. So when I met her for lunch one day and she described the family business, what I heard was, "My husband owns a porn shop."

And I was like, "Yo, that's insane."

Adding to the confusion was the fact that she's Mormon.

"I had no idea you guys were so chill," I said.

"You should come check it out!" she told me.

I was like, "I don't usually shop at such a place, but I'm happy to support you."

As our meal wore on, I had more questions. "Doesn't it affect your relationship? How do you really feel about this store?"

She looked confused. "You have a business," she said. "Does that affect your relationship?"

Around and around we went until finally she said, "I don't understand what the big deal is. He mostly sells trinkets, old things, some guns . . ."

Finally, we figured out that it was all due to a misunderstanding, and we had a good laugh. And I learned a new word.

Another such instance happened at work. Back before I started my business, I had a job as a director at a clothing company, and I had to attend a regional sales meeting. Part of our training was to go through a workshop where all our individual screens were projected onto a large screen at the front of the classroom. The manager led us through the various parts of the training, and at the end of each section there was a little box we were supposed to check.

When we finished the first section, the manager said, "Everybody check the box."

Then he said, "Tan, can you check the box?"

"I checked the box," I replied.

And he said, "Tan, will you actually check the box?"

"I checked it," I said. Because I had.

"Tan," he said. "Can you *please* check the box?"

By now you've learned that I have a short fuse. So by this point, I was like, "I. Have checked. The box. I have *seen* the box. I understood everything. Can we please move on?"

The manager came over to my laptop and pressed a little button that checked the fucking box.

I was like, "Ohhhhh. Tick a box?"

"What?" he said.

"Americans call it a checklist for a reason!" I said. I learned another word that day.

Though we speak English in both the US and the UK, there are definitely differences in our language, and Rob has experienced them, too. There is one moment from a decade ago that he's still not over.

On this particular occasion, when we were living in the UK, Rob and I were working together in the store. I was helping another customer, and a woman went up to the cash desk where Rob was standing and said, "Do you have this in another size? I'm an extra small."

Rob said, "Oh, really? Let me go find that for you."

He meant nothing by it, but in England, saying, "Oh, really?" is essentially the same as saying, "No, you're not, bitch."

The woman was not amused. She threw a hanger at him and replied, "Yes, I am. I'm a fucking size four!"

Rob was totally confused as to what went down. I had to explain to him, "In England, if you say, 'Oh, really,' it's like you're challenging someone."

He has never said it again.

Obviously, I find Rob very attractive, and thankfully, I've found him more and more attractive over the years. His style is wicked, and I want to grope him all the time.

However, the thing I really like above all else is his personality. That bitch makes me laugh all day, every day. I'm a very playful person, and I don't like to be serious, especially at home. I put music on and bop along as I brush my teeth. Anyone else would probably want to kill me, but Rob always plays along. We always keep each other giggling.

Though I've talked about the differences between the US and the UK, the truth is, when it comes to language, none of that matters anymore. Because Rob and I speak almost exclusively in a language we made up ourselves. Let me explain.

There's this comedy sketch show, *Little Britain*, where one of the characters speaks in this funny, almost Kermit the Frog voice. It's so stupid, but I started doing it once, and then Rob did it back. Now we speak this way to each other, and it warps words so much that they become new words. We've tried to do this in front of our closest friends, and no one ever has any idea what we're saying. I'm never concerned about people overhearing conversations with my husband, because no one will ever understand us.

Now, unless we are in the presence of other people, we speak this language to each other. We've been doing it for so long that when I hear him speak English to someone, I'll giggle to myself because I forget how he sounds when he actually speaks English.

I love that he's willing to be just as stupid and playful as I am and that he makes me laugh constantly. We do worry about what will happen when we have children. Does it mean we'll have to start speaking English again? What do normal people do? Are our children going to turn out batshit crazy? How will we raise our children to be decent humans when we are so childish? Even so, it's lovely to be in a place where cultural differences are overshadowed by the new culture we've created for ourselves.

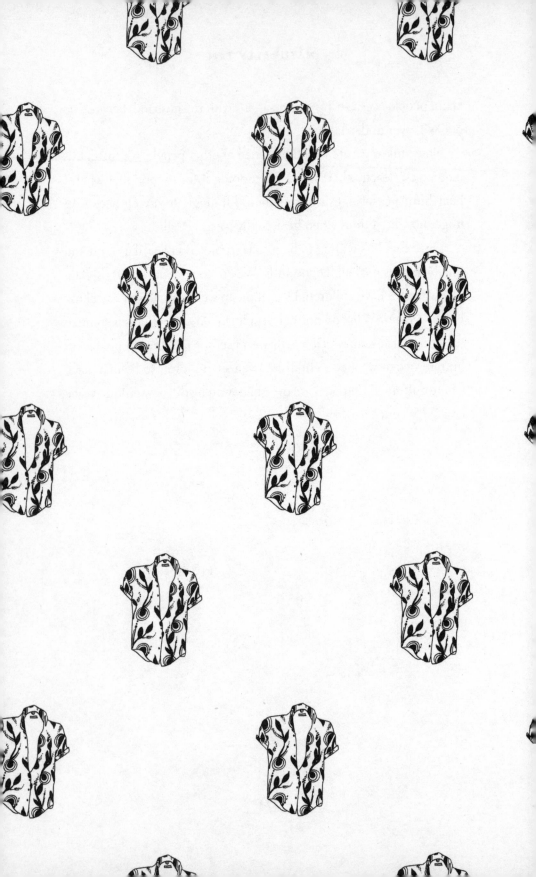

PRINTED SHIRTS

I want to dispel a common misconception.

Since the show first aired, there are a lot of people out there think-ing, *God, Tan loves a printed shirt! He wears colour and prints every day!*

Actually, I mostly live in solids. My everyday wardrobe is largely black, white, grey, and denim. But I had to step it up because I was on a TV show and the producers wanted to be able to spot us in a crowd. This meant lots of colour and, yes, printed shirts. Don't get me wrong; I love my wardrobe on the show. I do love a print, but I wear them very sparingly when not filming. My bold outfits are for the show, not what I wear in my day-to-day life. There is a difference.

If you're the kind of person who does want to stand out from the crowd and to change up your style by adding a little pizzazz, then a bold colour or print is a great option for you. However, I mostly like to keep pretty low-key when strolling around town, so I usually opt for more muted looks and keep prints for the likes of TV and events.

I also don't know how it became a thing that "Tan France only does floral shirts." Actually, ladies and gentlemen, go back and count. Out of twenty outfits, only *four* of them were floral shirts. When it came to dressing the heroes, the same thing was true. I only put them in *three* floral shirts. It's amazing how much that one thing stood out and I became the floral shirt guy. I actually do love how much of a thing that became, though. Any press is good press, right?

Why do we call them the *heroes*? Because these are people who wake up in the morning and decide to tackle the day. We can be our own everyday heroes. Just going out there and doing all you can do for those around you is a heroic act, in our opinion. They're showing up for their families or their wives or partners or whatever, and we don't want to belittle them by calling them *clients* when they are so much more than that. Everyday heroes.

About two weeks before we meet the hero, we receive a dossier about them, as well as a three-minute video from their audition tape. It's usually their nominator saying, "This is why this person needs help." They'll talk about the fashion, grooming, interiors, food, and cultural aspects of their lives. The dossier also has information on what they like, as well as what they absolutely don't like, so I can plan in advance what store I'm going to take them to. I'd love to live in a world where I can meet them and say, "I'd love to take you to wherever," but there's a lot of legal and logistical stuff that goes into booking a store, so we need to come up with a plan about which store I'll take them to.

Season 1, episode 1 (with Tom Jackson) was not meant to be our first episode, it was meant to be our little tester episode, because we were still finding our feet. It was to be an episode we could hopefully use somewhere in the season, but not the opening episode of our show. It was all of our first times on camera together, and for me, the scene where I meet Tom Jackson was *the* first time I had been on camera, ever.

Let me tell you, this is a shocking, shocking experience. Especially for someone who used to be uncomfortable taking a simple darn picture.

Based on the measurements in Tom's dossier, it seemed like he should be taken to a big-and-tall store. This was not the case. Tom is neither big nor tall; he is average size and average height. But Tom didn't know how to measure himself, so I was going with what info was given.

People who know the show will remember that we meet him in a diner with all the ROMEOs (Retired Older Men Eat Out), where they meet every Tuesday. What you don't see in this scene is that immediately after I say hi, I turn around to the producers and say, "He's neither big nor fucking tall. What can we do?" I'm standing there thinking, we planned a whole day at a big-and-tall store for tomorrow and I'm about to make my first major mistake and it's only my first week on camera.

I cannot take him to another store, because big corporate stores need at least two weeks' notice to get the clearances we need for filming. So instead, I take him to a vintage shop where I pick out a hat. Because that is my only option. To this day, I cannot watch that episode again, because it gives me the worst flashbacks. I'm immediately transported back to having that feeling of, "I'm going to get railed for this."

Here's the thing. What you guys don't see is the behind-the-scenes of the planning and the team it takes to make a scene work. So, when something seems slightly off in a closet or shopping scene, it's something that we've desperately tried to make work but have stumbled, and the person on the receiving end of the criticism is whoever is the face of the scene. Me. That was a really tough pill to swallow.

If something doesn't fit quite right, it's because that was the closest size we could get to the hero's size in the amount of time we had. Or the tailor wasn't able to hem all the jeans in the closet in time before the end of the scene, and the hero just so happened to choose the only pair of jeans that weren't altered to wear for his big reveal. Or we have an agreement with a store for that episode, so I can't put the hero in the outfit I ideally want to put them in, as I can only use the brand's specific options available to me. Or that's literally the best that the store has to offer, and I have to use a local store for the scene. Can you see how this can get really worrisome?

Every time something like this happens, I feel physically sick and pray that I don't get ripped apart online. It's so much more than just picking out an outfit that I love and then having the hero wear it. With my category, there are so many variables to consider that the audience never gets to see. Every hero is a different height and body shape. Every

School photo. I was around seven years old.
The only picture I have of myself as a kid.
Yes, my hair is naturally this curly.

2006, when my
hair was full-on
Justin Beibering.
I don't know why
I was taking style
inspo from a preteen?

At an Indigo
Girls concert in
Salt Lake City
around 2010.
I had no idea
who they were.

Rob and me, Manchester Piccadilly train station, 2008.
The first month we met.

Rob and me, San Francisco, 2011. The only thing I remember about this day was hating how bulky my hair had gotten at the front.

Rob and me, Buckingham Palace, 2008.
I straightened Rob's beautiful curly hair for this day. It was a mistake.

Rob and me near the Great Salt Lake, 2010.
I borrowed his shoes. I just need to clarify, these were *not* my shoes.

Rob and me with baby Oliver, 2011. The moment Rob knew I was going to want a *lot* of kids. Look at the nervous fear in his eyes.

Rob and me at a friend's fortieth birthday party,
Salt Lake City, 2010. I was living in Utah and
perfectly happy taking pictures with balloons.

Summer 2012. I was always a jealous bitch who looked great in pink.

Dinner in LA, April 2017. We four had been cast already. Waiting for Ant to be finalized.

After the final night of the second round of auditions, when we were trying to lock down the role of the Food and Wine guy. Clearly, we were rooting for Antoni.

April 2017, the final night of the audition process. We hadn't gotten the job at this point, but already you can see that a friendship had formed.

Antoni and me, June 2017. The hardest I've ever
seen him laugh, when he saw me in this wig.

With my *Queer Eye* boys, May 2017.
Our very first day in Atlanta, ready for preproduction of season 1, episode 1.

brand has its own version of sizing. Every retailer we work with has an agreement about what items they're willing to give us and what they're not. Maybe one day I'll get to do a "behind the scenes of *Queer Eye*" special?

The good news is, since Tom, I've never made that mistake again. The original dossier was pretty standard, but after that first episode, the dossier got far more comprehensive. I can't assume that a man who desperately needs help knows how to properly measure himself or what to ask for. Now we ask many more questions, including what colours they like.

I want to make sure each and every thing in that closet is right for my hero. But for me, the image is secondary, because the most important thing is their emotional transformation. The wardrobe is integral to everything I'm doing on the show. The emotional journey falls by the wayside if I can't do my job.

As for my own wardrobe on the show, for seasons 1 and 2, I was the only cast member who shopped for his own wardrobe. I'm given a budget, and I can buy my own clothes for the show. The other boys get options pulled for them by a stylist, and then they work with the stylist to put looks together. Do I get involved with the other boys' styling? It's definitely not my job, but I sometimes cannot resist. Sometimes Bobby or Antoni will ask what I think, and I'm happy to weigh in. Sometimes I give my very much unsolicited opinion. There were a couple of times during the first two seasons where I look back and wish I had said something, but I didn't. Will I ever tell anyone what these looks are? Absolutely not. I wouldn't do that to my boys.

While filming the third season, my personal styling choices came into question from the higher-ups. On episode 1, I wore a sweat suit, and in my opinion, it was fucking incredible. It was a grey oversized sweatshirt, which I belted and paired with grey sweat shorts. I've never felt so hot. Temperature and attitude.

The following week, I wore another sweatshirt, and it was called into question. The higher-ups were concerned that I looked too "casual" and "out there" and that I couldn't encourage the heroes to make an effort if all I was wearing was a sweat suit. It was an awkward conversation that lasted a few days. I explained to them that in fashion, you must first learn the rules, but once you do—once you understand proportion and how to style things—you can start to break them a bit. These looks weren't like I'd just rolled out of bed in my sweats. It was a very thought-out, intentional style moment.

"Maybe you could wear skinny jeans and button-ups again," someone suggested. "Like you did last year." Was I frustrated by this comment? I sure was. I don't love being told that what I'm wearing isn't appropriate when my wardrobe is the one thing I give a disproportionate amount of consideration. I don't want to be seen as a one-trick pony. I want to show range, and now I feel empowered to do so. I want to be young and play with style for as long as I possibly can. I'm not the kind of guy who's going to wear a suit every day, because that's not the only appropriate clothing option for men of a certain age. By that token, I'm also not going to wear a sweat suit every day, but I love having the freedom to toggle back and forth, depending on what I want to project to the world that day.

I talk about sweats a lot on the show, as in, "Don't live in your sweatpants." But if sweatpants are *intentional* and well proportioned and part of an overall look, I am a fan of that. I love the direction that fashion and style are going, for both men and women, in terms of being more casual.

Now, don't get me wrong—I do love a floral shirt, and I love a well-fitting suit. When you're getting dressed, sometimes I think it's nice to do something that isn't plain. Whenever you wear a printed shirt, you look like you put more style into your look. It was a considered style choice. Even though they're a trend right now, I don't think printed shirts will ever go out of style.

Polka dots and stripes will always help you perk up a look, and I do think we've hit a point where florals will be treated the same way. Perhaps a bold-statement floral isn't for everyone, but everyone can wear some version of it. Floral prints have been around since fashion began. When did it start, and when will it end? Who knows, but while it's here and a thing, I'm not hating on it.

There is no wrong time to wear a printed shirt, except maybe at a funeral—a floral shirt is probably too jazzy for a funeral. For any other occasion, there are ways to tone it down. The easiest way is to layer something else with it, like when you wear a printed shirt underneath a suit. It gives you a pop of something interesting, but you're only showing a smaller portion of it. It also takes a suit from being super corporate to being a style moment.

There was a time working on the show when I was worried my fashion/style scenes wouldn't be impactful. The shows are filmed out of order, so it's hard to get a sense for how it will all come together. The producers said, "We need print; we need colour," and I delivered because I agreed it would translate well on camera and in real life. Then they said, "Let's put them in a bright suit," and I put my foot down. Let's not get carried away. Because if people are truly looking to our little show for takeaway information, I want to make sure that what I'm putting the heroes in is real and can be useful to them. For me, this isn't just a TV show. It's a real experience, and I want it to feel that way for the audience, too. The pressure is on, and I want to make sure every single thing is right.

Is it sometimes slightly more outlandish because it's TV? Yes, but it's never something I wouldn't personally wear. It feels amazing to know that people have tried to imitate looks from the show, whether they're looks of mine or looks I've put my heroes in. People tag me on social media multiple times a day, showing their versions of my styling, and it makes me smile every damn time. I never would have thought that a decision I made would connect with someone from a far-off land, so much so that they'd post about it. I'm awed and humbled by it.

It probably (definitely) sounds pompous to say this, but after the first season aired, major fast-fashion retailers were selling their version of the floral shirt, and when I'd go shopping, it would look like they'd created a full-on Tan France section of the stores. Racks and racks of floral print shirts and mannequins styled the way I'd styled myself on the show. It was everywhere. Could my style impact the landscape of apparel retail? Gosh, I hope so.

After season 1, my biggest fear was that floral shirts were the only fashion talking point for me with the press and viewer—that nothing I could do would top it.

Then came the French tuck.

Nothing I've done in my adult life has ever caught fire like this. It is the most amazing feeling to be anywhere in the world—Australia, Asia, Europe, *anywhere*—and have people come up to me asking, "Am

I French tucking? Am I doing it right?" At one point, literally hundreds of people were tagging me every day, saying, "I'm French tucking!" I didn't think I could quantify it, but now I can. I hope it never gets old.

There is a lot of pressure around being the fashion guy. People definitely expect me to look a certain way all the time. I used to be able to go to the store with whatever I had on around the house, which—in fairness—usually is something clean, ironed, and well thought-out. But now, I have to dress up for anywhere I go. Coming up with a new look every day is the most pressure. Also, that shit's expensive, you guys.

Being in this industry is tough to begin with, but as a person who has built my personality around my appearance, I've really set myself up. I know for the rest of my life, people will be like, *"That's the style guy?"* and that's a lot of pressure. People aren't expecting Karamo's house to look nice or even for him to dress a certain way. They just expect he'll be able to listen and give solid advice.

You know that person who's trapped back in high school because that's when they were hot? I think that's my greatest fear. I don't want to get stuck in one trend or to be a slave to a certain moment in my life. Decades down the road, I don't want people to ever say, "Oh, there's Tan, French tucking his floral shirt."

The question I've been asked many, many times over is: Was it called the French tuck to begin with, or is Tan just calling it that because his last name is *France?* The answer is, it was always called the French tuck, but my gosh, it's a stroke of luck that my name is France and I'm known for the French tuck.

I've also used it for the last twelve years on almost every one of my outfits. I first saw it on the runways and thought it looked great, and I've loved the look ever since. It's my finishing touch, like a woman who wears lipstick every day. The French tuck is my lipstick. I've been using it forever, and I'm not about to stop now.

Now that floral shirts and French tucks have become a thing, there are other things I wish would catch on.

One in particular has been embraced by women, but I'd love to see more men in high-waisted pants, whether trousers or jeans. You saw men in this style in the '30s, '40s, '50s, and '60s, and even some in the '70s, but then it fell out of favour. It's very flattering. (As compared to a mid-rise, or especially a low-rise, which I think is very unflattering on most people.) Calm down, dear; I'm not talking about pants all the way to your rib cage, but somewhere close to your navel. Decades ago, this was seen as a very masculine style, and I wish it could make its way back into the mainstream. I'm wearing this style more and more, to try to encourage men to embrace it as a go-to style, but I think I might be fighting an uphill battle. C'mon, you guys, get with it. You'll be glad you did.

I love that people are taking information away from the show. We're living in a different world than in 2003 when the first version of the show aired. I thought, *Who would care about my styling suggestions on a TV show these days? It's 2018; people have access to Google and to social media—they don't look to TV for inspiration.* It's amazing how wrong I was.

I'm flattered that people are paying so much attention, but don't limit yourself to a TV show. One question I get asked a lot is where I go for inspiration. Finding inspiration has never been easier.

Go to Instagram, Twitter, or Pinterest. Search for hashtags, like #mensstyle or #mensfashion. Also: blogs, blogs, blogs. Men's and women's style blogs are incredible resources. Browse around online until you find a lifestyle blogger who has a style similar to yours (or a style you want to emulate).

One reason I always refer people to blogs is because the posts are bloody linked. Men! Don't wait until you get to the mall to go shopping. Use your resources. If you see a "click and buy" link on something you like, click it and buy it. Don't wait to try to find it in a store. Let's be stealthy about this, you guys. I promise you, this is the way forward. Technology doesn't move backwards. It's not like online shopping is going to get old and go away, so your only resources are malls again. That's never going to happen. Get with the (software) program.

"But bloggers make money off my purchases," some people balk. Yes, yes, they link to things so they earn a commission—good work; you caught them, Sherlock. The jig is up! Who cares if they earn a percentage? Let's not pinch pennies here. It's not like it's costing you any extra, and you're using them for their style advice. They're providing a service, so why shouldn't they get paid for it? As long as you end up with the items you like, just let them earn their darn fee, and let's not be so bitter about these bloggers. They never suggested that they were linking items or promoting products as an act of charity. They have mouths to feed, too.

If you're feeling real extra, and you want to step it up even more, follow the runways. You can see them all for free online, dating back like ten to fifteen years. That shit's expensive, but it'll give you inspiration for how to style things differently. I use the runway purely for styling inspo.

For women, Pinterest is mostly female driven and can be an incredible resource. However, you need to set your alarm; otherwise you can get lost in a black hole. I remember once I got lost in a Pinterest hole for like two fucking days. I looked up at the end of one eight-hour workday and thought, *Holy shit, I didn't even answer an email all day.* So maybe avoid that. Set your timer, avoid all the crafty shit—I may live in Utah, the home of crafty shit, but I am *not* a scrapbooker—and browse the inspiration for style, home, beauty, and food.

Men don't talk about it enough, but women talk about their favourite stores. People surround themselves with people they like, so ask your most stylish friends for their opinions. It's fine to ask someone where they like to shop or even to say, "Hey, I'm really struggling. What stores do you like? Can we go together?"

You've got the world at your fingertips! There is no excuse. Go out there and find your style.

TAN'S LIST OF THE BEST-DRESSED CELEBRITIES

When people say, "I don't know where to start!" this is what I tell them. This is my actual answer—find a celebrity whose style you love and Google photos of them for reference. "But, Tan," you might say, "these celebrities are dressing in fancy, fancy clothes, and I can't afford them." I get that, but if you go to the likes of Zara and H&M and Topshop, they'll have knockoff versions of the same things at accessible price points. For almost any everyday look you admire, I promise you can find an accessible version.

When it comes to inspiration, here are some of the stars I look to again and again . . .

Victoria Beckham

She is my all-around number one. It's crazy to me that now she is one of the best-dressed women on the planet, because back in her 1990s

Spice Girls days, there was nothing posh about it; it was a little bit "scary" spice. The fashion press would never have described her as stylish or cool. But now she's so chic, it's almost regal. She's incredible.

Tilda Swinton

Whenever there's a red carpet, she's the one I'm waiting for. Very few women but many gay men find her super stylish. I don't know what the problem is or why the rest of the world doesn't love her, because I think she is so cool. She can be androgynous, and she can go from super feminine to über, über masculine. I love that she's not following what everyone else is doing. She comes up with her own look and does her own thing, which is why she's a muse for so many designers.

Cate Blanchett

After I've seen Tilda, Cate is the next person I look for. She doesn't have to make a massively bold statement, because her elegance and sophistication are unlike anyone else's on the planet. She does occasion wear better than anyone else. In my opinion, she is the queen of the red carpet.

Cheryl Tweedy

As far as I'm concerned, she may be the most beautiful woman in the world. She encouraged and empowered women in the UK to dress more interestingly. She has a more playful, interesting version of style that isn't just supertight nightclub wear, but also rocking trainers and track pants.

Actually, side note, come to think of it, the most beautiful woman in the world is the queen of Jordan. That shit is insane.

Gigi Hadid

Her style is cool, and I admire that she changes it up every day. The luxury for women is that they can reinvent their look every day and be a new version of themselves all the time. Gigi takes advantage of this, and I really respect that.

David Beckham

I think he's one of the most relatable fashion icons for men. He's sort of an everyman, even though his beauty is otherworldly. He'll wear a simple jumper and boots and jeans, and he always looks chic as fuck. If you're a man and you don't know who to look to for inspiration, he's a really safe option.

Zayn Malik

When it comes to my own inspiration, I really prefer someone like a Zayn, who can do street wear really well and can do '90s grunge one day and a Balenciaga moment off the runway the next. It doesn't hurt that he looks incredible in everything he wears.

Justin Trudeau

As far as politicians go, he looks fantastic. He's showing men in politics how to wear a really well-fitting suit and how to command a room instead of looking like you've worn your granddad's clothes.

Russell Westbrook

Russell is an NBA player, but until literally a few weeks back, I didn't even know what sport he played; I just followed him for his fashion.

He's like no one else. I love that there is someone in this totes masculine sports world who is saying to men, "You can care about your appearance, and you can use fashion to express your personality." Expressing your creativity doesn't make you queeny or gay; it just means you care about how you're presenting yourself to the world. He's breaking down barriers when it comes to the intersection of fashion and sports.

CROPPED SHIRT

A few years ago, I was watching an interview with old-school Marky Mark, who obviously everyone has had a crush on at some point over the past twenty-five years. Even now, I can't think of anyone who doesn't think he's a little bit sexy. In the interview, he was wearing a sweatshirt that was cropped, and I thought, *I haven't seen a good crop in a very, very long time.*

Crops used to be everywhere. Can we please take a moment to talk about how bros were wearing crop tops in the '80s? *How* was that not more talked about? How was that not seen as gay then, but it is now?

You mean to tell me that nobody thought it was strange that all these jock bros were running around wearing crop tops, back in the '80s and '90s, when people were even more backwards than they are now?

Anyway, back in the present day, I was looking at Marky Mark's sweatshirt and wondering how I could incorporate that into my own look. So I found a sweatshirt and cropped the bottom of it. I left the sleeves long, as I didn't want it to look too costume-y. I didn't have the confidence in my torso to wear it sans undershirt, so I layered the crop top with a tank top underneath and was living for the layered proportions.

One day before our press tour, I stumbled across a picture of me in that sweatshirt, and it inspired me to start doing it again. I wore a cropped shirt once to a photo shoot, and since then, it has exploded.

Antoni was obviously super jealous (as he always is of me) that I was wearing a crop top, because he has that insane six-pack and wanted to show it off. So he started to crop his sweatshirts. I'm using this book to set the record straight: that bitch stole my look. Everyone's acting like he came up with it, when it was really mine (and the '80s') first. We can't treat me like I didn't come up with something just because I don't have abs like Antoni Porowski. I wore it first. I'm sick of this racism and preferential treatment.

One day, we were in New York City doing press, and Antoni and I went shopping. We were each buying sweatshirts, and I said to the sales associate, "Do you have a pair of scissors? We'd like to crop these before we leave the store." So we did, and then we posted a picture on Instagram of us in our cropped shirts, saying we were twinning.

Jonathan saw the photo and was so mad and immediately Face-Timed me. "If you don't bring me a cropped shirt, I am going to kill myself, and then come back to life to kill you both before killing my-self again," he said. So we brought him a crop of his own. At this point, all three of us were wearing our cropped shirts on the way to dinner in an always-packed New York City. As we started to walk down the street, so many people kept running up to us and saying hi. It was a lot of attention.

Jonathan grew frustrated. "What is going on? This is very much, very much."

"*Are you kidding me?*" I said. "We're walking down the street in matching fucking crop tops. You can't complain that we're getting too much attention when you are literally the reason it's happening. We have to stop twinning-tripleting." Since then, I have needed to remember that I can't twin with either of them anymore, or that if I do, we can only do it when we are not walking the streets of any major city.

Since then, I have seen raw-edge crop-top sweatshirts *everywhere*, and I'd like to believe I had some influence. Yes, my inflated sense of self is back with a vengeance. But I really do think that I helped propel this trend forward. So there.

Even if crop tops aren't your thing, cropped items can actually be very flattering. If you're vertically challenged, most stores sell items that cater to the average-sized person, and it can be difficult to wear them. Longer items will morph your proportions and distort them into things you don't want them to be. Wearing a longer jacket, for example, will make you look shorter and wider than you have to.

Getting dressed is all about tricking the eye. So, when I'm choos-ing lightweight jackets, I'll choose jackets that don't hit past my hip bone, which helps make legs look taller and leaner. If I'm wearing lon-ger winter coats, I'll layer a couple of shorter items to counterbalance.

As a five-foot-nine person, I'm actually average height, but my cast-mates are white giants and one Karamo, and I am dwarfed by them. So I have to use every trick in my arsenal that I can.

Here's how it usually goes: gays will start to wear something, it becomes a trend, and then ten years later, brosefs will co-opt it, and I'll be like, "You're behind the times." Perhaps this is what will happen with cropped shirts.

This is what happened with T-shirts. Gays started wearing tight T-shirts, but now meatheads have adopted that as their official uniform. Don't get me wrong—they're usually very buff and nice to look at from afar, but you wouldn't want to date that. There is something about a supertight T-shirt that screams, "Look at me!" It's a bit tool-y.

Whenever I see people in tight T-shirts, it's usually not forgiving. Gone are the days when sexy-sexy sells. I prefer a looser fit. I like when your features are highlighted, but don't show it all off. Maybe show off one thing. That is all. Something loose and only slightly suggestive is much sexier than wearing skintight clothes.

I think our preferences around fit, for anything, evolve over time. Sometimes the trend is for things to be more fitted and sometimes looser. When I was in my twenties, I would put darts in the back of all my tops so they would fit me closely. But over the last few years, I've loosened up, and so have my tops.

PSA: T-SHIRTS

When in doubt, always go for a crew neck. This is especially true for men.

The one exception to this rule is if you are heavier set or if there is no true definition at your neck. If you are one of these men where your head and neck sort of blend together, then you should go for a V-neck, which will give you the illusion of a neck and balance out those proportions.

If you are not one of these men, *do not* wear a V-neck. Douchebags (especially in Las Vegas and New Jersey) seem to gravitate toward a V, sometimes even a deep V. You look like a tool. No woman wants that V-neck guy. When I see your deep V, I know who you are without you having to say a word. I know that you are someone who is single and isn't a great date—though you believe you are, just as you also believe that you're dynamite in the sack.

A deep V had its place ten years ago, and if it ever does come back, run a mile.

The wearer of the deep V sometimes teams the shirt with bedazzled jeans, or jeans with white contrast stitching on dark blue denim. If you see that combo, *run*.

For any men mourning their V-neck, sometimes people tell you things you don't want to hear. Sometimes your family and friends aren't strong enough to tell you, so Tan France has to do it. I'm doing the work of every single woman out there who's had to go on a date with someone dressed like a tool and is like, *I knew I should have swiped left.*

For women, I don't have a hard-and-fast rule. I still usually prefer a crew neck, but a V-neck can be nice with décolletage. With women, your neckline doesn't make as much of a statement of "tool or not a tool." You are the lucky ones who aren't defined by your T-shirts.

LEATHER JACKET

My very first fan interaction was with Jon Fucking Bon Jovi. He was literally the first famous person who knew my name. I cannot tell you how weird it is when you go from having absolutely nobody know who you are to suddenly being recognized by Jon Bon Jovi.

Our show came out on a Wednesday. Two days later, we pretaped *The Today Show*. At this point, the show had only been out for like forty-eight hours, and nobody knew who we were. On the streets of New York, there was no recognition. Even the people in the green room who were prepping us to go on air had absolutely no idea who we were. It had only been two days; of course no one knew our names yet.

I stepped out of the green room and into the hallway, where I started chatting with a producer named John. That's when I saw Bon Jovi and his entourage walking down the hall. He looked slick as shit with his leather jacket and salt-and-pepper mane. To be honest, I'd never considered myself a fangirl for him, as he wasn't as big a star in the UK, but he is a legend and his songs are iconic. Everyone knows who he is. I hadn't really met anybody famous at that point, and this was a huge deal.

I had never been one to stalk a celebrity before. I stood there talking to John the producer, thinking, *Ignore Bon Jovi. You have no right to say anything to him. You are not his friend. You do not know him. He doesn't care that you're on a show. Why would he? Let him go on with his life, and act like he's not there.*

I had my back turned to him at that point, because I didn't want him to think I was staring. I heard his footsteps stop.

Then he kind of touched my arm and said, "Do you mind if I get a picture?" I thought he was asking me to move out of the way so he could take a picture with John. I stepped aside.

He was like, "No, Tan, can I have a photo with you?"

I gasped. I was like, "Wait, what? You know my name?"

And he was like, "Of course I do! My wife and I love you on the show!"

I said, "Jon Bon Jovi, you can have whatever you want! Of course you can have a photo!"

He told me to call him *Jon*, but I said that my mind simply wouldn't let me do that, Jon Bon Jovi.

I turned to John and said, "Can you take a picture of me and Jon Bon Jovi?"

And so we took some pictures. There's one photo where he's

putting something in his pocket, in between shots, and my mouth is wide open and my expression is one of complete and utter shock. What the fuck was about to happen to my life?

"Since I can have whatever I want, can we FaceTime my wife?" he asked. "She would love that."

At this point, the other boys noticed what was happening, and then they wanted to get a picture, too. (Jon Bon Jovi forgot to FaceTime his wife, because the boys totally screwed that up, and I never got to talk to her. Did I mention that I hate my stupid boys?) We couldn't believe somebody famous knew who we were. From that point forward, everything snowballed out of control.

Those first couple of months, every time we would see famous people, they would be so excited we were there. I never in a million years expected these people would ask *me* for a picture. "Do you mind if we take a picture real quick?" they'd ask. *That's my line. I'm little Tan from fucking South Yorkshire, and this makes no sense. Why are you asking me for my picture?*

At this point, it happens virtually any time we go somewhere. It's an incredibly strange feeling. I don't think I'll ever be regular Pakistani Tan from South Yorkshire again. It feels so surreal. I would love to be cool and act like, "Oh, it ain't nothing." But no. Freak your shit out. Some things are worth freaking your shit out over. I've trained myself to remain relatively composed. Know this is a lie. Inside I'm my teenage girl self, experiencing a full-on mind explosion.

No matter how many times this happens, and no matter how weird my life becomes, I will never forget that moment with Jon Bon Jovi and thinking, *My life changed today.*

It has just kept changing, ever since.

CROSSED LEGS

I've always thought of myself as quite effeminate. But as a younger person, it was something I really tried to hide for fear that I would be called out.

The other day, I was having a conversation with Jonathan and Karamo in the trailer, and I mentioned how effeminate I was. They started to laugh. I said, "Obviously, JVN and I are the most feminine in the cast."

And then they played a little game. It wasn't malicious; they were just trying to make a point. They said, "Let's put everyone in order, according to how feminine they are." They put me near the end, right before Antoni, who came last. Apparently, I'm not quite as effeminate as I thought.

I think I used to give myself a harder time than necessary about it. Even as we discussed it that day, we talked about how insignificant that notion seems now, especially in this position we are currently in. I'm not trying to hide the fact that I'm gay anymore. So it doesn't really matter if I'm feminine.

In my early life, the only concern I had with seeming feminine was that people might know something I might not want them to know. Still, every now and then, a little voice rings out in my head: *You are South Asian—this isn't how you behave!*

The voice had a lot to say when we did the show *Lip Sync Battle*. We were told we could dress up however we wanted and sing whatever we wanted to do. The boys said they wanted to do a Britney number— to start with Beyoncé and then go into Britney. I would have gone with something hip-hop, because that's what I prefer. Don't get me wrong— I love me some Beyoncé; I just didn't fancy doing a pop song. But I was outnumbered; we would do Britney. Then there was a costume fitting, and we were trying to decide which character I would play. This meant one thing: I was going to have to do drag.

Until then, I never saw myself doing drag. I had never even con-sidered doing it before. I've watched many a drag show, and I find it hilarious; it's just never been something I have a desire to do. I've never felt a desire to wear a dress or a full face of makeup or a wig. So for me, it wasn't something that excited me.

I was hesitant.

When it came to the costumes, we got to choose which version of

Britney we wanted to be. Before anyone else could comment, I said I wanted to be Circus Britney, because she wore flat boots, and I didn't want to dance in a heel. She was also relatively covered up. Of all the options, it seemed like it was as much like me as physically possible while dressed like Britney Spears.

Our outfits were decided five days in advance. Then we turned up the day before the live show and the costumes were already made and fitted. They tested our wigs and makeup, and we danced in our outfits to make sure things didn't fall off.

I always thought you'd have weeks and weeks to prepare for something like this. You do not. We had three hours the day before to rehearse and then the next day we had one hour to prepare before they filmed. For me, four hours does not a dancer make. You could have given me four days and it wouldn't have made a difference. I barely slept a wink the night before, because I wanted to make sure I knew the moves.

When it came time to film, Antoni and Bobby screwed up the cue and did it way earlier than they were supposed to, which made me look like I didn't know what I was doing. But it didn't matter, because it was all so much fun. Everyone was lovely to work with and made us feel great. It was an incredible experience. If I could do it a thousand times over I would.

Still, it's weird looking at pictures of myself in that outfit because I'm not used to seeing myself in a full face of makeup. I would make a terrible drag queen. Antoni looked really pretty; he would make a great drag queen. But Bobby and I looked pretty damn scary.

It frustrates me that people would think, *You're gay! Why wouldn't you do drag?* I'm not ashamed of myself. If you're straight, you don't automatically have to be into NASCAR. Maybe it's not your thing. And just because I'm gay, I don't have to enjoy every stereotype involved with being gay. I've had to remind myself time and time again that I don't have to do anything. I can be the version of gay that I want to be. There are parts of gay culture that definitely aren't me, and drag is one of those things.

In the end, I enjoyed it, more because of the overall experience than because I was in drag. But it did remind me of the fact that if I naturally have feminine traits, that's fine. I don't want to feel like I have to force feminine traits just to be part of the gay community. Nor do I want to hide them.

I wish our society could be more open when it comes to masculine displays of affection. I remember when I was eight years old and first visited Pakistan, it was the first time I saw guys holding hands, and I thought it was really weird. I wasn't aware of my sexuality yet. But I did find men holding hands to be very peculiar. My brothers and I would giggle and joke about it. We had never seen anything like it before! These were grown men holding hands.

I look back and think, *Gosh, that's really evolved. They're comfortable enough with men letting down their walls and saying, "I have affection for this friend. This small show of affection brings me closer to my friend in a way that is not sexual."* They understand it doesn't have to mean anything other than that they are friends and that they care for each other.

Even now, I don't hold my husband's hand in public. I fear that it could lead to someone saying something disgusting or that it will lead to a situation where there might be an arrest or an altercation. I hate that I feel that way, but I do.

I do think there is an issue with masculinity in this country where it's gone way overboard. I think stereotypical masculinity is a super archaic notion. There is no place for it anymore, especially in America. I'm talking about the kind of masculinity where you feel the need to display it.

If you feel secure in yourself, then holding your best friend's hand to show them you care for them shouldn't be a big deal. It seems indicative of a bigger problem if someone feels they can't be openly affectionate with friends—even if you're just in private.

Despite my feelings about this, I don't hold the other boys' hands in the street. I would like to—it's a sign of affection. It's really sad that people twist it around and try to spin it into a story about an affair or use it to suggest that something more is going on. Believe me, if something were going on, I'd be a lot smarter about it and would try to hide it!

There is such a thing as friendship between two gay men. If you see two women sitting together giggling, you don't automatically assume they must be sleeping together; they can just be great girlfriends. It's sad that this can't also be the case for two men.

My level of comfort with my masculinity and femininity is ever evolving. These days, it's something I feel a lot more comfortable with, but it wasn't always the case.

Growing up, I was really skinny, but I wanted to put on more muscle. As a teenager, I asked my doctor so many times, "Is there anything I can do to put on weight?" I would eat like a pig, but nothing would happen. It still infuriates me that I can't put on weight. I've been working out since I was twenty-one, and I work out six days a week and eat as much as possible, but still, I'd love to have a more masculine body.

Most days, I'm not massively concerned. But I think more men need to have conversations about body image. I'll have crazy times, like when I have to wear a swimsuit in front of other people, where I'll feel mortified.

I actually don't show my body in public. I haven't gone swimming since the show aired, because I think there is this misconception that if you're a man—particularly if you're a gay man—you're supposed to be ripped. Do I feel self-conscious now more than ever? Yeah. Am I likely to go to a public pool any time soon? No, I am not.

Recently, I was in Hawaii with my husband. I was in a swimsuit on a desolate beach, and still, someone wanted to take my picture. I explained I don't like to have my picture taken with my shirt off. It reminded me of why I don't do this. I don't want to give the internet trolls a reason to attack me. Putting my body out there for the world to see feels, to me, like giving everyone an opportunity to discuss me on a level that I don't feel comfortable with. They can comment on my personality or what I do for work, but when it comes to my body, I would be very hurt to hear opinions on my physique. Even the positive comments ("Oh my gosh, you look so skinny") can be not what I want to hear. It's just a self-protection that I feel most people wouldn't voluntarily say, "I want to put this picture on the internet for millions of people to critique."

Do I long for the day when we finally get a pool put in our home? Absolutely. Really looking forward to that.

The sad thing is, I think everybody should be able to show their body publicly! I think that I put this kind of pressure on myself because the entertainment industry puts this pressure on us. I do think there is a belief that a young gay man should look like an Adonis.

In season 1, episode 6 (Remy's episode), there was a scene where I crossed my legs while wearing short shorts. I was so worried about what people would think of me. "Uncross your legs!" I kept yelling at the screen. We've been conditioned to think that to be desirable, we have to play masculine. I hated that I had internalized that so strongly.

But finally, I had to have a come-to-Jesus moment. I had a conversation with myself where I said, "You shouldn't pretend to be masculine if that's not you." There are both feminine and masculine sides of me, and I realized I shouldn't have to pretend or to hide who I am.

Sometimes, I would catch myself crossing my legs or having a limp wrist, and I would stop myself. But finally, I thought, *You are on a show. You are on a gay show. You are on* the *gay show. The jig is up! Also, who cares if boys don't find you attractive? You're a married man!*

It took me a long time, but I'm so happy that I'm finally in a place where I no longer feel the need to whitewash or straight-wash myself in order to fit in. But some old habits do remain.

This morning, I was at the gym, and I didn't notice that Jonathan Van Ness was also there, on the treadmill. I was finishing up and walked behind the row of treadmills, and he ran after me. "It's funny how you walk—totes masc at the gym," he said. "You've got this, like, gym bro walk."

I didn't realize I was doing it, but I was like, "Gosh, maybe I do walk differently at the gym." I trained myself early on to avoid any kind of confrontation, not to advertise, not to create a scene. And I hate that it—even subconsciously—is still a thing.

Initially, I walked in whatever was my natural way, but along the way, I must have learned to walk a certain way from women on TV and in movies. Apparently, I developed an effeminate walk when I was very young, and I remember family members saying, "Tan, don't walk like that. Boys don't walk like that." I would try my best to walk like a boy, walk like a boy, walk like a boy, but I was hyperconscious of it.

I took it so far that I remember, in high school, people saying I walked like a rapper from Compton; I had apparently gone so far beyond my natural walk that I tried to be a cool young black guy from the hood. I had to find a walk that felt appropriately me, and that took years.

Being on the show—and also being surrounded by gay men—has reminded me of the fact that I shouldn't try to be anything that I'm not. We encourage people on the show to be their authentic selves: "You do you!" "Don't hide yourself away!" "Don't hide your feminine side, show off who you truly are . . ."

I remember saying these things and feeling like a complete imposter, because everything I would encourage someone to do would be something I also struggled with. I would think, *You didn't do any of that until you got this position.* I've always encouraged people to live authentically, but I understand all too well how it isn't always easy. For me, the journey to self-acceptance has been a long one.

NOT-SO-FANCY LUGGAGE

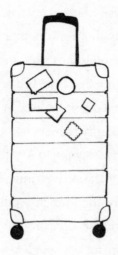

So often, my friends and family mention how I now lead this glamorous life. You pose for the camera! You go to New York every week! You go do international press! It all looks so glam.

When we first started doing press, it did feel glam, and I felt like a pretty princess. For about one week before season 1 was available, we made our first appearances on US shows like *The Rachael Ray Show, The Wendy Williams Show,* and *The Today Show.* It all felt so glamorous, because I'd seen these shows for years and we were doing things that famous folks do. I was so impressed by it all. I thought, *Ooh, ritzy glitzy, Tan. You must be something to get on a show like this!*

But then we were on a press tour from the start of February until pretty much when we started filming season 3. If we weren't flying somewhere for press, we would be doing phone interviews (what we call *phoners*) for two to three hours every day. It turns out that really, there is nothing glamorous about sitting in a hotel room for days on end, being asked the same questions over and over. And every time, you have to fake it like it's the first time you've heard that same intrusive, embarrassingly personal question, like "What did you think when you first went to [insert celebrity name]'s home?"

Then we found out we were going to Australia. When you find out you're going to a foreign land, it's very exciting. But when you get there, you realize all you'll see of the foreign land is the hotel room, the inside of a car, and the inside of a pressroom. Don't be fooled. If you ever get on a show and you're lucky enough to do an international press tour, it means you will see a long flight, the inside of a hotel room, and a car. Australia, New Zealand, Dubai, London . . . it's all the same because you're in a hotel room. Don't get me wrong—I couldn't be more grateful for how much press we do for this show, as it means we're doing something that people want to talk about, but it really isn't as glamorous as I'd thought it would be.

The best part of going an international press tour, though, is that you get to sleep like you've never slept before. You're constantly on the go in this industry, so fourteen hours away from everyone and everything was the very best treat of all. You can't do any of the usual stuff you would do, because the Wi-Fi doesn't work over the ocean. So, with the luxury of a first-class seat, you sleep and catch up on movies. Now that, my dear readers, is the most glamorous thing of all, in my opinion.

I love that the press has been so supportive, and I'm shocked by how positive they continue to be about us boys and the show. But the truth is, at a press junket, you sit in a room, sometimes for up to ten hours, and every fifteen to twenty minutes, someone new will rotate in to ask you questions. Every reporter thinks his or her questions are brand-new, yet they have been asked hundreds of times, and keeping up the energy after you've been interviewing for three or four hours is very hard work. You get this weird, fuzzy-headed feeling. There is a ringing in your ears, and you feel like you could fall asleep at the drop of a coin. Yet you're expected to be the same version of yourself that you are on TV.

But imagine flying on the longest flight you've ever taken and—within an hour of landing—getting dressed and ready and then performing at your highest level for up to twelve hours. Imagine if you didn't even have half an hour to decompress. You have to hit your hotel room, get your face on, and then sit in front of the cameras.

It's stress-inducing, because whenever this happens, I'm not on my game. And then when the reporters ask questions, I'm far more likely to say something that I definitely don't want to say. For example, they might ask questions about a certain episode that hasn't come out yet, and I'll slip and offer information and only afterward think, *Oh, shit, I wasn't supposed to give that away.* And I know my PR person is going to be furious that I've let something slip.

Or I might feel so tired that I accidentally give away information about a friend, because I felt so tired that I forgot to pack my emotional arsenal. Or they'll ask what I think about a celebrity or someone's new movie or someone's new song, and because I just want to get to the next question, I'll give a too-honest answer. Then they'll try to create drama between us.

All of it is just really exhausting.

I am so lucky to have four other castmates, because we've learned to work in sync with one another. We each have different tells. The other boys know I'm getting tired when I start to stutter a lot. This is for sure my main giveaway. For Antoni, he gets this vacant look on his face. It will become very obvious to each of us when one of us is struggling, so the rest make up for it. Then someone else will drop off, and we'll readjust. I can't imagine being on my own on a press tour; it would be hellacious.

Everyone expects to see "Tan France from Netflix's *Queer Eye!*" at all times. But the Tan France on the show has usually had some time during the day to decompress. He hasn't been in a room for ten hours, not seeing sunlight, expected to answer the same questions over and over again, acting excited the whole time. It's a tough act to keep up when all you want to do is not speak for a couple of hours and just decompress.

The best way I can describe it is this: Imagine, if you're married, your wedding day. You make your way around your wedding party, all day, making sure everyone is having a great time. If you're fretting about something not going to plan, or you hit a wall and are exhausted, you know you still have to power through and pretend like you don't have a care in the world because today you have to present your very best self to everyone at that wedding. It's tough.

Going back to London on our press tour was one of the most wonderful experiences of my life. I was given a hero's welcome (it sounds arrogant to say, but it's true!), and I've never felt more proud to be British. Going back to England and being able to say, "I represent us," felt so fucking epic. There aren't a lot of us British personalities out there representing the global community. Every major show and every news outlet treated us, and especially me, beautifully. It felt so impactful.

I never dreamed that I would get to be on the likes of BBC Radio 1 or *This Morning*. Radio 1 is massive in the UK. It's just as popular as the biggest shows on TV. When I was first told that we were going on, I practically screamed the house down. Rob couldn't understand why radio was so important to me, but it was. It was a part of my young adult life in England, where I listened to it every day.

As for *This Morning*, my family had been watching that show since before I was even born. It's like our version of *The Today Show*. To appear as a guest was insane. I took three of my closest friends from the UK: Nas, Kiri, and Vicky Downie—and it felt so special having them there to witness how wonderfully exciting this had become.

The trip was over before we knew it, as the five days were jam-packed with press, but it was truly magical, and I can hardly wait to get back over there again.

When it comes to press, another thing I love is an editorial. Do I love a magazine shoot? Yes, I do. If I could just do editorials, that'd be great. The actual features can get really meaty, and you get to do a photo shoot. I live for a cool photo shoot.

When it comes to editorial, it's all very sane and organized. There are no surprises. The magazine discusses the concept with you beforehand, and you start to plan looks with their stylists. When you get to the shoot, they treat you like you're a star. Someone is there to greet you at the door with the coffee order your manager gave them earlier, and then it's straight into wardrobe, where you get to play dress-up and decide on who you want to be at that shoot.

One of my very favourites was *PAPER* magazine, as I got to show a side of myself I'd never shown before. I wore full makeup for the first time, my hair was styled in ways I've never tried, and my clothes were over the top in the very best way.

Then, as the music blasts—I usually choose Nicki Minaj—the photographer starts to shoot and call out directions, all while telling you how amazing you look. All this is to say: magazine shoots are like a fantasy where you're the queen for the day. It's the best.

Press is, without a doubt, the hardest part of the job, not only because of the energy required to perform for hours on end but also because of how much it impacts your life. With press obligations, you usually find out just a couple of days in advance, and you have to change all your plans and fly somewhere very quickly. It makes it difficult to have a regular life. I know I sound like a spoiled brat, because I'm in a very privileged position, but it's hard to plan things. I had to cancel attending my good friend's wedding—which I'd planned for months in advance—because I had to do press. I cancelled my husband's fortieth birthday vacation because I had to shoot something last minute. I missed my niece's wedding because I had a work obligation. That's just the way it is. It's an incredible life, and I feel very blessed, but you miss out on a lot of real life. There is no way of saying no; if you're on a show, you're bound by the commitment you've made.

Sometimes, you'll also run into situations that aren't great. There will be green rooms that haven't been updated since 1982, or a city that isn't so glamorous where you're in the middle of nowhere, without a coffee shop or a drugstore or really anything in sight, or a hotel that's terrifying.

Also, when it comes to life in hotels—and this is a big thing—it's super lonely. I'm in a place I don't know well and where I don't know anyone. After a long day of press, I go back to my hotel and order room service. If I go out, I'll just have to perform all night, so I stay in my room all alone. I miss my friends, and I miss my husband. It's a lonely, lonely place. Usually, I'm missing Rob because I haven't seen him in days and days and sometimes weeks and weeks. We don't have the kind of marriage where we want breaks from each other. We loathe time apart. And being away from him really brings me down.

At the end of a long day, I'll walk into a hotel room and, no matter how lovely it is, none of it really matters because I feel lonely. I'll brush my teeth, looking into the mirror and thinking about how much I wish I were at home with my husband in the other room. Then I'll climb into bed and think how much I want to be going to bed with him instead of alone, once again. And I'll wake up a thousand times in the middle of the night thinking I just want to feel the comfort of my partner next to me. I'm so grateful to get to go to so many incredible places, but I wish I could do it with him. I'm also the kind of person who gets homesick very quickly. Even when I'm traveling with Rob, after a few days, I want to be at home, in my own bathrobe, getting ready to go to sleep in my own bed.

Now that I've sufficiently whined, let me assure you, there are definitely points of a press tour that are amazing. Our trip to Australia is one example. We were there for four days—we landed at night, and first thing the following morning, at 7:00 a.m., we had to be up for a junket interview, which is where you sit in a room for eight or ten hours while journalists rotate in.

When you go on a press trip, you know your schedule for the entire four days, and there is no time to explore. You can explore from the car on your way to an appointment, but otherwise you won't be able to see anything.

Yet we had flown for twenty hours, across the world.

So that first morning, Jonathan and I woke up at 5:00 a.m. We watched the sunrise and took an hour to explore. One of the most magical moments of my life happened there in Sydney, where Jonathan and I walked down from our hotel to the harbor, and we danced and watched the sunrise.

We were so excited to be in Australia. My god, it was exhausting, but I was so grateful for that trip. And I'm just as grateful for every trip I go on. Yes, no one wants to sit in a press junket for ten hours. But those moments remind me how amazing life has become.

We do all we can to find those magical moments to remind us of how special it is that we even get to go on a press tour. There are so many shows where no one gets a press tour. It's amazing to have that opportunity and that I even get to be in a foreign land with the people I love.

So definitely don't pity me. I think I've sufficiently tried to make you feel bad for me, to make myself feel more grounded, but don't fall for that shit. Other than the press stuff, it is pretty glam. Waaaaah.

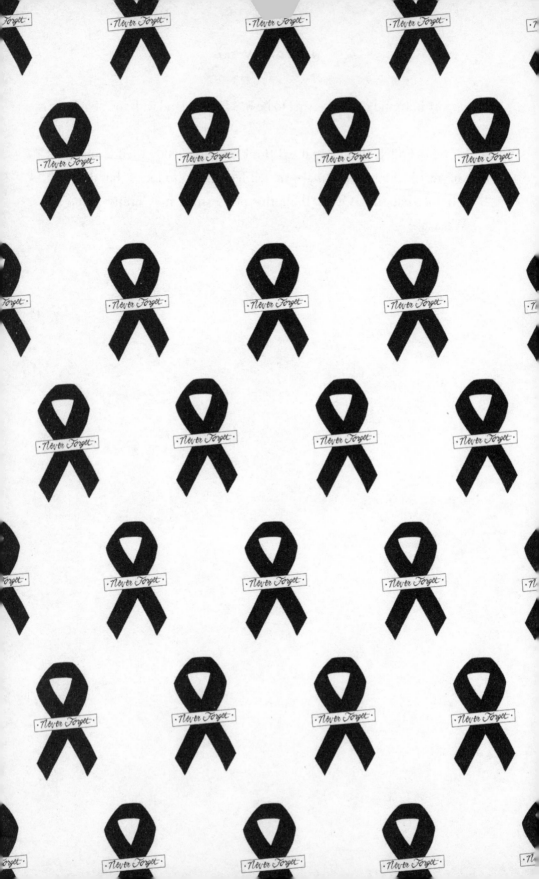

9/11

·Never Forget·

I'd like to discuss September 11. I know this is a really awkward subject for many people, but I feel like it's high time some of us started to talk about it. For many years, I've hidden behind the American perspective, and now I'd like to give the brown perspective. Audience, please bear with me.

On September 11, 2001, I was working at the call center (where I met Dave) and I remember exactly when it happened. It was 4:00 P.M. there, and I'd just arrived at work for the evening. When I walked into my little area of the call center, everyone was acting weird. Our office had this massive screen that played the news, and when I looked up and saw what had happened, my reaction was, of course, "That's terrible."

And then, things started to change.

Over the course of the next few days, everything started to feel a little strange. For the first time in a long time—since I was a young boy—I noticed that people seemed to look at me differently. In the coming weeks, there was a shift. I heard people saying things about me. As a kid, I'd grown used to people calling me a Paki, but now, for the first time ever, I was being called a raghead or a terrorist.

A terrorist? I had never even considered the idea that someone might see me that way. It felt worse than anything I'd been called before, because not only were they saying, "We hate you because of your skin colour," they were also saying, "You're a threat." How could it be that even though I had been raised in the UK and was just as British as anyone else, I was now seen as a threat? It was a weird adjust-ment.

No matter how I tried, I couldn't understand it. I couldn't make sense of my own feelings around it. It made me feel obviously "less than." I felt more alone and more "different" in the eyes of the white community than I ever had before.

It also really pissed me off. After all, my community was just as angry and just as worried and just as scared as everyone else. Yet because we were brown, people expected we should feel fine because it wasn't "us" they were coming for. For anyone who might think this, that's not how it works. Terrorists do not discriminate. If the US or the UK got attacked, we would all be targeted.

Over the years, I have also experienced white people waiting for an apology. When encountering South Asians, Middle Eastern people, and Muslims, white people have said, "There are terrorists out there causing real damage. Why don't you apologize for that?" Why would I apologize for people I've never met? If a white guy down the street blows something up, I don't see all white people apologizing for him.

When I was a teenager, I visited New York for the first time, which was also the first time I traveled without my family. I was pulled out of the security line at the airport and taken in for additional screening. Meanwhile, my friends walked right through the security line, but had to wait for me while I got the special treatment. This is a trend that has continued over the years.

When you pull up to the United States customs desk, they have a way of making you feel like garbage before you've even said a word. If you're me, they tell you that you'll have to go to another room for additional screening, and it's all very confusing. The holding room is full of brown people—from all different backgrounds, but all of them brown. It is so glaringly obvious that one time, a blond girl walked into the room and said, "Oh my gosh, I must be in the wrong room." We all laughed, and she turned around and walked out.

To date, being held in the special room has happened to me at least twenty-four times.

I know it sounds like I'm playing the race card, but sometimes the race card needs to be played. When you've spent most of your life being repeatedly sent to a room that is entirely full of people of colour, you cannot ignore it.

When I first started regularly traveling to the US, people would say to me, "Why do you keep going there? It's clear they don't want you. They keep putting you in a detention center." This was a fair point.

After you've spent time in the holding room, you are called up for questioning. "When was the last time you traveled to Pakistan?" the officer will ask. I can't imagine the last time a girl from the Valley was asked that question. I've only been there a couple times in my life. So I say, "When I was nine." Then they'll ask, "When was the last time you operated heavy machinery?" It's absurd.

The first time this happened I was really offended. I tried to be polite and agreeable, in order to make it out of the room as quickly as possible. But after a few times, I felt comfortable being sassy. Now I'll say, "I already know what you're going to ask. I came from the UK. I haven't been to Pakistan since I was a child. What's in my suitcase? Gay magazines. How many gay terrorists do you know? I haven't operated heavy machinery lately. In fact, I never use heavy machinery, but I can operate a sewing machine. I can make you a very nice dress if you like."

One time, on a trip to the US to visit Rob, I was coming through the Chicago customs desk with a visa waiver that said I had up to ninety days to stay in the United States. But the customs officer arbitrarily decided he didn't like me, and he said, "You only have seven days." I don't know who gives them this power, but it's a lot of power to give someone.

I replied, "I have three months."

Then he looked me in the eye and very clearly said to me, "You are not welcome in this country."

He also slowed down his speech as though I couldn't understand English.

I said, "First off, you do not need to slow your language down for me. I speak English very well. Second, I am a model citizen, and there is no need for this."

Thankfully, I could petition his decision and was granted an extra few weeks with Rob. But it's alarming that I've needed to deal with this as many times as I have.

This treatment continues until this very day. I was stupid enough to believe that the job I have now might put me in a position where someone might say, "He's not a terrorist. He's Tan." But no. There is no club you can be part of where you will be exempt from this.

To be clear, I don't expect to receive special treatment. I am happy to go through the same process as everyone else. But to be pulled out of line at the airport, and to be seen as a threat—I wasn't expecting that. It's mortifying. The entire line of people behind you is being held up, all the while thinking, "What has this brown guy done? Why are all these TSA agents gathering around him and searching him?"

Now the experience is magnified by the number of people who recognize me. I'll be getting interrogated, and all these people are taking photos like, "Oh! Look! Tan France is being searched again!"

When I travel, I usually wear a cap to disguise myself. But when you're being searched, you don't get to wear a cap. So while this is going on, people are getting all these pictures of me with my hair not done, which might be the worst part of all! While TSA officers are searching me, people stop to say hi and ask to take photos, and I have to be like, "I'm being treated like a terrorist right now, can you give me five minutes?" It's incredibly stressful.

Because I think this is something people should be aware of, I posted about it on my social media and the press picked it up. At first

I thought, "Good. More people need to hear about this. We have every right to say we're being profiled." But my worry is that if we speak out, the profiling and interrogation might become even worse.

Every year, on the anniversary of 9/11, and in various places around the United States, I see the words *Never Forget*. I understand that sentiment. I completely agree with honoring those who lost their lives. We must never forget them, and we must always be vigilant. But there is another side to this, too. It means we never forget to see my people as a potential threat. We haven't stopped racially profiling. We haven't realized that when it comes to the events of 9/11, and any other potential threats to our countries, these feelings of loss and fear and anger and tragedy affect all of us, regardless of the colour of our skin.

WALLET

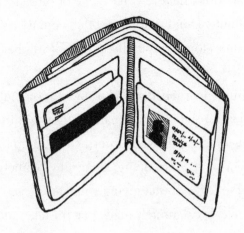

I want to talk about what it's like to go from being a regular person with a regular income . . . to becoming wealthy. Yes, I'd like to go there. I know it's an awkward thing to discuss, as finances aren't usually up for discussion, but let's do this. This isn't necessarily about becoming "Tan France from Netflix's *Queer Eye*," as these are rules I followed before then. But they continue into my life today.

Having access to large amounts of money, when you once had little, can be a shock to the system. I think it's important to take a beat before deciding how you want to spend it.

When I started to earn more money, I didn't make a lot of major changes in my life. In fact, for the first few months, I didn't make any changes at all. I didn't buy a house. I didn't choose the most expensive car I could find. Because I know that even when anyone is lucky enough to have a burst of success, in any industry, it could fizzle out. Life may seem amazing sometimes, and you may feel like you're invincible. But whenever I have one of those feelings, I try to breathe for a minute. Don't move to another country or even another city. When it comes to major purchases, they'll still be available in a year or two.

Another thing I learned is to keep my mouth shut. Being met with success doesn't mean you've earned the right to be opinionated about things you're not overly informed on, or to have thoughts about what other people are doing, especially publicly. No matter your position, I've learned that giving your unsolicited opinion is a way to hurt people. I've definitely made that mistake, and I will never forget it.

Once, during an interview, I was being pushed to give my opinion on many celebrity outfits. I'd avoided saying anything negative for almost all of them, but the interviewer was becoming frustrated that I was being too nice about these obviously crazy looks, so when we reached the final example—a look with super short shorts—I said I loved it but that it was way too bold a look for me to pull off. I actually meant it. I thought it was great—for him. It wasn't a look I could rock, as it wasn't my usual style. But the person found out and reposted the quote on his Instagram and seemed a little hurt by it. Thankfully, I sent him a DM to apologize, and that cleared it all up. Still, it taught me to never do it again. I wouldn't want to be on the receiving end of someone's mean comments, so I don't want to make those comments. (And no, I won't tell you who the person was.)

Do I have opinions on everyone's outfit? Of course I do! That's my job. But they don't need to hear that. No good can come of that. I now try to think of how I would feel if someone commented negatively on something I was doing or wearing, and that's enough to make me shut my damn mouth.

I've learned that when you get a lot of money, it doesn't mean to go ham. Yes, it might be nice to upgrade a bit, but don't go batshit crazy. I've kept my lifestyle relatively similar and try to save more money. Making more money means your taxes will be higher. Be responsible, and resist the temptation to spend like a crazy person. Because otherwise, if the deals dry up, you'll have nothing to show for it except for your misguided impulse buys.

When you haven't had a lot of money for much of your life, and then suddenly you get a lot of money, it's easy to think, *I deserve this!* and to spend it. Yes, you may be great and talented and all those things, but I always remind myself that nobody deserves this. Nobody. I am blessed. I can't take it for granted.

One rule I learned early on is that spending can get out of control quickly and can put you in a financial bind. That extra $100,000 you didn't have before? Spend maybe 20 percent of it. The rest, keep on hold.

It's kind of the same with people who are newly famous, where their fame spirals out of control very quickly. You never know how long things are going to last. Sometimes, a person is seemingly everywhere, but then you don't see them again after five years. Where do they go? Who knows. But wherever they are, they'll need cash. Slow your roll, because I'm sure you won't want to go back to your regular nine-to-five job you had before all of this happened. (Remember, I love an "I told you so.")

Even though my life has changed so drastically, I actually haven't changed my lifestyle very much. I still spend relatively conservatively. The designer clothes you see on my body on red carpets are borrowed. When you see celebrities on the red carpet, or when you see us at a party or a runway show, those clothes that we're wearing—those things that might be $10,000 or $20,000 or that jewellery that costs a fortune—we don't usually own that. We also don't get to keep that. We send most of it back to the company. Occasionally, at a photo shoot or a fashion show, the designer will let you keep a piece, but that is the exception. On the whole, you give it back.

If you want to live like a celebrity, please know that even celebrities don't live like celebrities . . . if they're smart.

The nice thing about life now is that I'm in a position where I don't have to worry very much about financial things anymore. It's a luxury I am truly grateful for, and it makes me count my blessings every day. When I was younger, I was told money doesn't make you happy, but let me tell you, I think it's only disgustingly rich people, the kind who have been rich since childhood, who think that money doesn't make things easier. Don't get me wrong—you can still have real problems, but it's nice to not worry about your rent and bills. It really is. And before all this, my stresses were way more daunting when my bills were also a concern.

It's also nice to be able to take care of your friends. I enjoy knowing it's not an issue to pick up the bill or to send them whatever I want to congratulate them when they get a new job or have a new baby. One of my favourite things to do right now is to spoil people I love with things I know they wouldn't do for themselves. I would never have arranged a spa treatment or a massage or sent myself a massive birthday cake, but I like to be able to do it for my friends.

It's lovely to be able to spoil my husband. It's lovely to not have to even give it a second thought if I want to fly him somewhere. Now that I live away and travel a lot, I want him with me. The network or press doesn't fly him wherever I am, but it's nice to be in a position where I can say, "You can cut back at work and be able to spend time with me." My husband doesn't need me to provide for him and would never expect me to. I love that he wants to work. I find ambition and a good work ethic very, very sexy. But it's nice to be in a position where if he didn't want to work, he wouldn't have to. We're incredibly lucky.

I've also learned to be careful of new friends. I know this is just common sense, but I've become more guarded since the show came out. I love meeting people, but I don't let people into my life too much, unless they have the same sort of nondisclosure requirements that I do. It's a self-preservation thing that one simply has to adopt to protect oneself when you enter the public eye.

The one real negative about having more money or relative fame is that other people feel entitled to some of it. Suddenly, you have people coming out of the woodwork telling you, "I'm working on a project and struggling to drum up funding," or "I'm having a hard time paying off this thing." I find people sharing these everyday things, which they definitely wouldn't have told me two years or even six months ago. Or they'll feel entitled for you to post their project on your social media for no real reason.

If I authentically love the thing that you're doing, I will post about it. If a friend or a family member needs help, they'll have it. But when someone is trying to take advantage of a situation, it feels uncomfortable. You start to see that person differently, which is a shame.

My real friends are people I've known for years. I love them, and I know that they love me for me. The quickest way to lose my trust in friendship is by asking to take advantage of my work. That's a downside I wasn't expecting. I think anybody who is in this industry or anybody who has acquired wealth probably experiences this, and it's really hurtful. I'd like to believe I would never do that to a friend, and so it's harsh when someone does it to you and puts your relationship into question.

I love that you might be asking in my DMs if we can hang out. "We both live in Utah; can we go for dinner?" but the answer has to be no. You wouldn't send that to any other stranger, so you shouldn't send it to me. It would be highly unwise of me to say yes, to think that since we live in the same state, we should be best friends and we should go to dinner. You've got to understand that doesn't make sense.

I love when people feel like they have a connection with me, but making friends with somebody I've never met before is a huge risk. Will I be so happy if I meet you in the street? Absolutely. Will I smile and give you a hug and be thankful? Yes. But I'm the most boundaried person in general, and now I really have to be. I love and I trust the friends that I have. They're my rocks, and I know they'll be with me when all of this is over. They're ride-or-die bitches.

I'm not massively concerned about fancy cars, homes, jewellery . . . those things don't faze me. I'm not a materialistic kind of person. Of course there are some clothes or a bag I'll think is nice. But then I'll look at the price tag and think, "That's about a month's wages for my family," and I'll get an icky feeling. I pray I never get over that. I would feel I'd lost myself if I spent a fortune on things I would wear once, knowing that could make a difference to a family member's entire year. So I'm sticking with what I know and appreciate—accessibility. Does that mean I won't happily go to a major designer show and support their art, or borrow a piece of designer clothing for the red carpet? No. I still love me some fashion moments.

In my early to midtwenties, I used to say, "I'll know I've made it when I can fly first class every time I fly, not just for business." For me, that was the mark of success. Does it still feel that way? Kinda. As soon as that happened, I was like, "Okay, I'm going to be all right."

I feel very, very lucky to be able to fly first class, especially if it's lie-down; it absolutely makes a difference to my travel experience. I will say, though, even now, every time I get to board first and get into my seat, I think, *Little Tan would be freaking his shit out right now if only he could see this.*

NATURALLY TAN

The reaction to Netflix's *Queer Eye* has been very positive. For me, this was relatively unexpected. Up until this point, there hasn't been another South Asian person on such a grand stage, and the support hasn't just come from the South Asian community but from all communities.

Within a few days of the show airing, I had hundreds upon hundreds of comments from people thanking me for being me. "Thank you for not hiding any aspect of yourself!" Whether it's the gay side or the brown side, it's true that I am completely myself.

Now, all over the world, I get to hear people tell me how lovely it is to see themselves represented on television. Recently, I collaborated on a video with the comedian Hasan Minhaj, and while we were at a press event, I saw a brown journalist sit there smiling the entire time while watching the video. He said, "This must be what it feels like to be a white person watching TV. To see yourself." It's not that the people you see are exactly like you, but you know they understand you on a certain level. You feel represented in a different way.

And when he sits there smiling, I truly understand how he feels. When I watched our show for the first time, even though I was watching myself, I felt represented. I thought, *This is surreal. I'm not playing a taxi driver, I'm not playing a terrorist, I'm not playing a doctor. I'm just a regular Pakistani guy whose voice is heard.*

When I saw the movie *Crazy Rich Asians,* I loved that it was one of the highest-grossing movies of the year with an all-Asian cast. It just goes to show you, just because the lead isn't white doesn't mean a project won't do well.

I hope that our show and others like it continue to open up more options for people like me. Why can't the lead or the heartthrob in a movie be a person of South Asian descent? Why can't they cast people from all different backgrounds, not to fill some diversity quota but because a person from a different pool can be desirable also? I hope that increased representation can continue to encourage the idea that beauty doesn't just belong to Caucasian people. Not just in terms of physical beauty but in terms of everything we have to offer.

When I was younger, I struggled with this idea. Whenever a child is born in the South Asian community, the first question people ask is, "Are they fair?"

This question—about whether the baby's skin is light coloured—comes before anything else, even before inquiring about their sex. I've heard it so many times from family members.

"Oh! Aisha just had a baby!"

"How fair was the child?"

I've heard it a million times, and everyone else in my community has also.

Or an elder will turn up and say, quite openly, "Gosh, they're cute, but they're very dark." Then they'll immediately offer little tips and tricks—like covering them with turmeric paste—to try to lighten them up.

People assume being male is important—and it is—but that question comes second. Only after you've determined whether or not the baby is fair-skinned do you determine whether or not the baby is a boy. People want their firstborn to be a son, which is archaic. But being a fair-skinned male is the best.

As a kid, this will fuck you up.

It's a really weird thing in the South Asian community, but it's not unique to ours. I've seen it in the Black community, in the Asian community, in the Middle Eastern community . . .

It's amazing how people of colour can be some of the most racist people you'll come across. It's not because they fear or hate other people of colour; it comes from a place of status and class, and how you don't want your place to be misrepresented, and from subconsciously assuming that white is "better" because there are greater opportunities for white people.

From a very young age, I was frightfully aware of my skin tone and how it "should" be fair, and how if it weren't, I wouldn't be in good social standing. I had been conditioned by the subconscious beliefs of my family and the people around me, and South Asian media at large, to believe that if I wasn't fair, I wouldn't have a happy life. There's a belief that if you aren't pale, you won't get married because no one wants to risk having a dark-skinned baby.

One of my best friends in the UK is Bengali and has beautiful dark skin. One of my family members saw us together when I was a teenager and said, "That's fine if that's just his friend, but she'd better not be his girlfriend, because they might have dark children." (Little did they know!) Never mind that this is the most stunning woman you will see! To this day, I know people back home who are single and still lightening their skin because there is a belief that, in order to get married, you need to lighten as much as possible to increase your desirability.

We want so desperately for our children to marry someone who is white, but they must not marry an actual white person. "Find someone who is pale as snow," we are told, "but she must identify as South Asian."

The importance of being pale is very bizarre. The people around me certainly didn't intend to pass on this belief, but I was aware of it and affected by it just the same. Culturally, you'll see white people on TV, you'll see a plethora of billboards in the Middle East and in Asia that are focused on lightening or bleaching your skin. When I was five, I remember thinking, *God, I'd give anything to be white. I just want to be white, I want to be white, I want to be white.* I had been so conditioned to think that if you were white, you were automatically more attractive.

I wasn't dark, but I did hear comments about others from my extended family. So when I was ten years old, I used to bleach my skin.

I actually stole the cream from one of my cousins who used it often. To this day, I haven't had the balls to tell her I took it, because, since then, I've been ashamed of the fact that I succumbed to the pressure. No one else knew I was using it. I didn't want family to know, as they were so sweet and accepting that I knew they would have stopped me because they thought I didn't need it. I kept the dirty little secret to myself. I'd only use it at night, before bed, when no one else was going to catch me.

Let me tell you, that shit hurts.

Around the same time, there was a girl named Rachel in my class at school who used to go on holiday every summer and get so brown. To this day, I've never seen a white person get so brown. When she got back from vacation, so many people were envious of it. I remember thinking, *White people* love *this shit. So maybe I'm not the devil because I'm brown?* Thankfully, I matured, and the bleaching wasn't something I wanted to sustain.

Now, if you ask me what my favourite thing about my appearance is, I'll say my skin. I think my skin colour is beautiful. As a ten-year-old, I could never have imagined that you could find my skin colour beautiful, and I'm willing to bet most nonwhite people have thought the same thing. That is a sorry state of affairs.

Sometimes I still have thoughts like, *I shouldn't sunbathe*, or where I'll look in the mirror and think, *Gosh, you look dark*. That's a shitty thought to have. *I shouldn't go outside today*. No one should ever feel that way.

Growing up, the other kids made fun of my siblings and me, and it came from both sides. The other brown kids would say we were coconuts—brown on the outside, white on the inside—because even though we were brown, we sounded white. At home, English was our first language, unlike a lot of the other families in our community, who learned Urdu or Hindi or Arabic first. We also watched a lot of Western TV shows, like *Saved by the Bell*, and because of this, our vocabulary was more expansive than the other South Asian kids in our community.

On the phone, you can usually tell if someone is South Asian, but with me and my family, there was no way of knowing. The other brown kids said I sounded like a white person and made fun of me in a playful way.

Meanwhile, due to the colour of our skin, we weren't accepted in white culture. So we didn't quite fit in anywhere.

My parents thought if we perfected our English and could sound as non-regional as possible, we would be better off. In England, if you have a very strong regional accent, people sometimes assume you're not well educated. I saw value in sounding non-regional from a very young age, because your accent does hold some weight, especially in the UK job market. Now, the one question I get from English people more than any other is, "Where are you from?" because they can't figure it out based on my accent. Whenever I hear this, I'm like, *Well done, Tan.*

My untraceable accent has occasionally caused some confusion in negative ways, as well. I was once told, "You speak English very well," by another English person. I remember saying, "Are you fucking kidding me? Of course I speak English well, I'm English." I think it was meant as a compliment, when really, it was so incredibly offensive.

People can be just as offensive in the US, too. Back when I worked at Shade, I often ate at a place called Taco Amigo, a little standalone fast-food joint on a busy street in Pleasant Grove, Utah. I usually ate with a colleague of mine named Caroline, and the same woman was always behind the counter to greet us.

I went there almost every day to order my lunch, and every single time, she spoke really slowly to me.

"Hi, how are you?" I'd say.

"Iiiiiiii'm fiiiiiiiine," she'd reply. "Howwww arrrrre youuuuu?"

"I'm well, thanks. May I please have a taco bowl?"

This is the part where she wouldn't only speak slowly to me but would also use Spanish words.

"Whaaaaaaat kiiiiiind of *pollo* doooo you want?"

"No chicken. I'll just have the beans, thank you."

"Are you suuuuure? No (pause) meat? (Pause.) Ve-ge-tar-i-an?"

"No, I'm not a vegetarian. And, as a reminder, I speak very good English."

This is the part where she finally spoke in a regular tone.

"Oh my gosh! I forgot! Every time I see you, I forget that I can speak English!"

These instances were such a casual version of racism; it was insane. You could knock me down ten pegs with just that one thing, assuming I needed someone to slow down for me. It was a real kick in the dick.

Finally, one day I went to Taco Amigo and the woman did the same thing, and at this point I'd had enough. "I just need you to understand that I speak English better than you!" I said. "And you are slowing me down."

I got the same exact reaction as I'd had every other week ("Oh my gosh! I forgot! I thought I was helping you!"). I knew that she wasn't being malicious; she was just culturally insensitive. I also knew that if I ever went back, it would happen again. So I never returned.

To any person who speaks differently to someone else just because they aren't white, I have to say, you deserve whatever response you get.

I do feel hopeful that we're moving in a positive direction. We've got a heck of a long way to go, but if you asked me twenty years ago if I thought something like our show would happen in my lifetime, I wouldn't have thought it was possible. Even when the original *Queer Eye* came on the scene fifteen years ago, if you'd asked me what would happen if they took away Carson Kressley and threw in a South Asian man instead, I would have told you that wasn't a show that anybody would watch.

When I was growing up, there weren't *any* people in the media who were my colour and also seen as desirable. I'm so glad that we're now finally getting to a point where more kinds (and shapes and colours) of people are being celebrated. There are more South Asian people on TV now than there used to be, but I'd like to see so much more of it.

When we did our press tour in the UK, Karamo pointed out how much more colour was presented in ads and media in the UK, and in Europe in general. We would notice so many people of colour in various campaigns, and it felt much more balanced than here in the US, where there will be a predominantly white advertisement with one token person of colour. It's like they're trying to meet their quota. I think a lot of times, the media will think, *Well, we've got a black person, so we've covered all the bases!* But having diversity doesn't mean just one black person. It means *multiple* people, where all races are represented. Until we get to that point, we don't need to call out, "Well done, everyone!" What about Latinos and Middle Easterners and Asians?

I'm so fucking glad that I'm on a show that's been met with so much acceptance from so many places, because I want it to be seen by kids who can say, "Tan's on TV, and he's doing fine. People want to shag him, so maybe they'll want to shag me, too." I would have killed to have had that when I was a kid. Just because I'm brown, that doesn't take me out of the game.

I hope that in my lifetime, a show like *Queer Eye* becomes archaic. I hope that there comes a time when there is no need to talk about being queer or gay or Muslim, when "Me Too" is no longer a thing, and racism is no longer happening. I pray we get to a time when all of this feels obsolete.

DMS

On a typical day, I receive anywhere between five hundred and eight hundred direct messages from people on Instagram. Most are lovely, and though I don't have time to answer the majority of them, I will answer as many as possible each day. Then there are always a handful—certainly not the majority—that are not so nice. And these questions get asked over and over and over again. Here's what I fantasize about saying, if I weren't trying to be so inoffensive all the time . . .

Where do you get your highlights done?
How? *How* can you think these are highlights? Look how short the sides of my hair and my beard are. There's no way I could keep up with highlights on those. No, these are not highlights. I'm just getting old.

Why do you think it's okay to be so affectionate with the other boys when you're a married man?
Ugh, thank gosh you were considerate enough to ask this in such a

nonjudgmental way. I'm so glad you asked about my marriage and what works for us. My marriage is, of course, your business, completely. But now I have a question for you: Why can't I be affectionate with the other boys? Women aren't judged for being so affectionate with their friends, so why can't I be so with my friends? This question says way more about you than it does me.

Why does your accent sound fake?

That's because it is. I'm actually from a small town in Alabama, but I learned to do a wishy-washy North England accent many years ago and used it to land the job on *Queer Eye*. I'm now stuck with speaking this stupid way forever.

Why don't you just stick with fashion and being gay instead of getting political about a country that's not even your own?

Oh my gosh, I can already tell that you and I going to be great friends. You think because I'm on a show, that's all I have thoughts about? That I can't possibly have other opinions because I've chosen my career and we're only allowed one discussion point—fashion? Do *you* ever talk about politics? And if so, do your friends ever tell you to STFU because you're actually a banker/teacher/plumber/whatever and so that's all you're allowed to have an opinion on? No? Then STFU.

How can I nominate my dad for the show?

I promise I have no control over this. I wish I could help, but all I can say is that the lovely team at ITV Studios does the casting, and we legit don't get to know about our heroes until a couple of weeks before meeting them on the show.

I'm going to a wedding next week, and I don't even know where to start. Could you send me links to options you think could work for me?

I love you for feeling so connected with me and my opinions on style that you would come to me for help, but I truly get this question literally twenty-plus times a day and already have almost every hour of my day filled with shooting, press, travel, photo shoots, keeping up with social media, and being a husband, sibling, and friend. Watch *Queer Eye*, and I'm almost positive I'll give a close enough suggestion for your occasion or requirement on there. Again, I love you. Thank you for responding so well to my style suggestions.

You didn't create the French tuck. It was created by women and repackaged by a man. You.

You're right, I totally said that I invented the French tuck. It's something I said in every episode and every interview. I insist on it being a quote used in every article about me. I'm surprised it took someone so long to catch me out. Call the fashion police. You got me. You know me and the gays. We're always trying to take down women.

You wouldn't know good style if it slapped you in the pompadour.

This one actually made me proper LOL.

Where are the other boys?

I literally don't know. We all live separately and have very separate lives. I love them and see them as much as I can when we're in the same city and not working, but when not at work, my guess is as good as yours, love!

TUXEDO

Everyone has that fantasy when they're a kid like, *What if I became famous one day?* Stranger shit has happened, so why not? Weirdly, in my fantasies as a kid, I was becoming famous as either a pop star or an actor. Weirder still, I can't sing for shit, so I should have known that was never a possibility for me and moved on from that delusion. Still, I would think, *If I were famous, how would it feel? Who would my friends be? And how would they become my friends? Would my manager reach out to their manager and set us up on a friend date?*

I love the show *30 Rock*—in fact, I watch it every morning as a way to start my day. When we're filming, Antoni and I will watch it together whenever we have a free moment. We're constantly quoting lines from the show. It's one of the many things that brought us so close together.

In one episode, the character Jenna Maroney starts to date James Franco. He's actually in love with his body pillow, but the relationship is set up by his manager to throw the press off the crazy man / body pillow relationship rumors. That's the way I imagined such relationships happened, where someone behind the scenes orchestrates the whole thing.

But now I can tell you that no, this is not the case.

Here is how famous people make friends: they slide into your DMs, just like everyone else. I know. I know. Who knew?

People you never in a million years would dream would know your name will just pop up unannounced in your direct messages and say, "Hey, do you want to hang out?"

It's so weird to receive DMs from people who are megastars, saying, "Hi, Tan! Do you want to come over later?" Yes, bitch, of course I do. You crazy? You think I'd have the bollocks to say no to you? It's so bizarre. It's also strange being summoned. When I first came out on the scene, I was fine being summoned, because I felt like lowly Tan who should be grateful that showbiz has allowed him to be a part of the scene.

When I first started getting contacted by celebrities, I would say yes to everyone. It was so interesting to see these people treat me like their equals even though some of them had been around for years and I was so new to the game. But as time has passed, I've gotten more perspective, and I realize I don't have to say yes to everyone. These guys are just regular folks when the glitz and glam is gone, so I should know that there are some I will get along with better than others. It's wise to be more selective.

When people from other reality shows contact us, I get that they would watch us. They're in the same game. But it's always shocking when it's an Oscar winner or when it's a performer who's legendary and whose music I listened to when I was a kid. That shit you never get used to. That still feels insane to me.

There are some people whom I desperately wish would slide into my DMs. Do I dream Adele will do it? Yes! I pray for that, I think, more than I do my own health. But I'm positive she's too cool for that, and for me. Still, there are other major stars who have reached out, and they're the ones where I'll stop and think, *Ho-ly shit, I can't believe this is my life.*

The weird thing is, I had thought, *I'll always feel out place when I'm around these people. I'll always feel aware that they are superstars and I'm just Tan from South Yorkshire.* But once you get to know them, you start to see them as just regular friends and acquaintances. And the bigger our show becomes, the more I start to realize that no one loves to be treated like you can't have a regular conversation with them.

I don't know at what point famous people are no longer regular people, because I'm still very much dweebo Tan. I wonder if I will always feel that way, or if I will become a celebrity and act too cool for that shit. But I hope I never do, because I love that feeling I have now. I love feeling like I managed to sneak into the coolest party in the world and I'm yet to be caught out.

My life has changed in many positive ways. I'll have access to shows or opportunities—like when I'm able to go watch a live taping of *SNL* or be on an episode of *Crazy Ex-Girlfriend*. It was always a dream of mine to visit *SNL*, and that was a thrill. The energy backstage is incredible. Everyone is pumped to give the very best performance. I remember feeling like I just wanted to jump on set with them. It was all so exciting.

But life has changed in many less positive ways, as well. It's not necessarily a negative, but I'm not really able to go out and about freely anymore. I promise I'm not moaning about this, because I actually find it funny. The amount of times my husband has turned to me in those situations and giggled after the person stops for a pic and says, "It's just dummy you; I don't get what all the fuss is about!"

Jonathan and Antoni love me very much until we're together in a city. Then they hate me. They mostly hate me for my hair and my skin, which makes me instantly recognizable. At this point, it seems rather impossible to walk around and act like I'm not that queer guy off the telly.

For the first few weeks of the show, I thought I could just put a cap on and nobody would know who I was. But I discovered it serves me no purpose whatsoever. People still recognized me, so what was the point of hiding my beautiful hair? Waaaaah.

When we're in New York especially, we cannot walk without it taking quadruple the time to get to our destination. We can only go from a place to a car to another place. There is no such thing as a public outing without being stopped every twenty seconds. The bigger the show gets, the less I can walk around *anywhere*.

Still, people stopping us on the street is beautiful. They always have the nicest stories to tell about the show and how it's impacted their lives—the dialogue in their homes, their relationships with their families. Connecting with these people feels so, so profound. It makes me feel like we're not just a TV show, we're more of a social movement. I like to live in a bubble where I can pretend no one's watching and that if I say or do a stupid thing, no one will see, and they definitely won't quote me back to myself. But of course, that is not true. Pretending no one is really watching makes it way less stressful a process. When I take a moment to think of just how many people are watching each episode and know me rather intimately, it gets me nervously sweating.

My favourite thing is when somebody shouts, "Hey, Tan!"

I'll still stop and think, *Oh, fuck, do-I-know-you, do-I-know-you, do-I-know-you?*

Until finally they'll say, "You don't know me. But I know you!" Oh, thank gosh.

And the craziest thing is that they *do* feel like they know me. I get a lot of hugs and also a lot of lifting. Like, *literally lifted up in the air* while being hugged. I'm the small one on the show, so I get lifted up a lot. But lemme say this. I'm actually five foot nine, which is average in the UK and the US. I'm really not that petite. (You would never dream of lifting Jonathan up; he's six foot three.) The lifting is definitely not my favourite. I'm an affectionate person, but I don't like getting to second base with a stranger. No more lifting me up, please, guys. It's way too much body contact for me.

I was one of those people who would roll my eyes when celebrities say, "I'm just a regular person." *You're not just a regular person! You live a proper glam life, and I will never understand,* I'd think. My god, was I wrong. Now that I'm in this and people behave in a similar way on the street, I just want to be like, "No, man, I'm just regular old Tan. I'm the same person I was seven months ago." But I don't, because I remember how that feels. When people I meet are super nervous and shaky and they drop their phone because they're so anxious, I want to say, "I'm the same as you. I'm just lucky enough to have this as my job."

The truth is, if you run into me on the street, know that I'm about to go home and eat ramen and watch *The Great British Baking Show*. Nobody will text me—I won't get a text all night, other than maybe from Jonathan. My everyday life is pretty simple, and I usually don't do anything remotely what you'd expect of someone in this business. Simple dinner, TV, and in bed by 10:00 p.m.

The other thing everyone needs to learn is how tagging works on Instagram stories. Many people think when you tag someone in a story, it only goes to their friends. But *I can see that*. I *do* see that. And when people tag me in a photo, it's usually when I'm stuffing my face, or mid-squat at the gym, or doing something that I probably shouldn't be, or else wouldn't want to be, photographed doing. I'll check my phone at brunch only to find someone from across the way has tagged a video of me. But I love calling people out. I'll hold up my phone, and they'll be mortified.

One of the first times this happened was a few weeks after season 1 aired. I was at a packed brunch spot, and while waiting for the check, I checked my phone and saw I was tagged in a pic by a guy at the table across from us. I looked over at him and held up the unflattering photo of me, fork in mouth, and rolled my eyes. I caught him, and he was mortified. Ahhh, it's the little things in life that give me pleasure.

Another thing people love to do is start rumors. If I go somewhere with Antoni, people love to suggest we're on a date. They'll post a photo of us to send to their friends, but sometimes they'll accidentally DM it to me. "Are you saying two gay men can't be friends?" I'll ask. "Let's talk about it." I love to call them out on that bullshit notion that two gay men can't just be friends.

I remember once I was out at a restaurant with a close showbiz friend's partner. Whenever I eat out, I try to face a wall to minimize the exposure, and this day was no different. But still, people noticed us. I hadn't seen his partner in a few weeks, so I held his hand for a second to tell him how much I'd missed him. Before I knew it, the big thing that day on my IG was that "Tan is sleeping with this person's partner." Even online publications posted the pic. It was so stupid.

Honestly, at this point, I find these accusations funny. The boys and I mostly giggle at them, and we laugh at how stupid they are. But I can see how, after a few years, it can really grate on people. I have a newfound sympathy for Amanda Bynes. I get it now. I want to send her a note for all the times I've used her as punch line. It was a dick move, and I can't tell you how ashamed of myself I am for that.

It's also weird to go from having no show to being approached to do other shows more regularly. I thought *Queer Eye* would be the only show I'd ever do. I never thought this could be a career option. It's lovely but also terrifying. There is a lot of self-doubt and a lot of ego involved in doing this, and it's a version of myself I've never known before. It's amazing how quickly your perception changes into "I want this, I need this." I keep meeting aspects of my personality I haven't encountered and wondering, *Do I explore this? Do I quash this?*

Most of the time, I question whether I'm even cut out for this industry and if I'm actually entertaining on camera. I sometimes worry that people gave me the job to fill a diversity quota. I sometimes worry that I'm not young enough to be seen as cool or interesting or worthy of starting an entertainment career at this point in my life. These things nag at me from time to time, and I have to remind myself that I'm in this job for a reason and that all I can do is focus on doing the best work I can. And when my time in this industry is up, I hope I can walk away knowing I tried my best to be as good as possible at the job while I had it.

Everything moves so quickly, I sometimes don't have time to process it. Every day, something major happens and there truly isn't enough bandwidth to process any of it fully. I really should journal more, so when things do calm down, I can look back and figure out how I really felt about it all.

Never in a million years could I have pictured everything that's happened. First of all, that I would even get the job but also that the show would become what it's become. I thought it was a crazy pipe dream of the creators thinking they could make lightning strike twice.

The original *Queer Eye for the Straight Guy* was a pioneer, and it had a fundamental effect on gays in the industry. But they did it again with our show. I never thought it was possible. I thought it would be a cute niche show that maybe some gays would watch, and maybe some girls, but not that it would achieve critical acclaim.

To be asked to present at the Emmys—to win Emmys—that blows my mind. Did I ever expect to win Emmys? Hell no. Here's the thing: I assumed the show would get a nomination because of what it represents. I thought it would be a really bad move not to nominate us for anything, because we represent diversity like I've never seen on TV before. But I truly didn't think, for even a second, that we were going to win.

We knew that the nominations were being announced in August.

The cast and some of the producers decided we were going to meet in a room in the apartment building where we were living in Kansas City and we would wait for an announcement. One of the producers kept clicking Refresh on the page.

We saw we were nominated for Best Structured Reality Program. We jumped and we screamed, and all of us cried. Up until that point, I didn't think I cared about an Emmy. I was just surprised to even be in this fucking business. But when we realized we had been nominated, it hit me. I thought, *I live in America. I've been nominated for an Emmy. I've been nominated for a show that talks about gay people. I'm a brown person, and I'm being recognized for being me.* It made me cry so hard. I never thought in a million years that I would feel pride like that.

I had so many feelings and so many thoughts running through my mind, and it really made me emotional. I stepped out of the room and called Rob on FaceTime, and as I cried, I told him, "Oh my god, we're nominated for an Emmy." Then, as I was on the phone, I realized everyone in the room was screaming again. We had been nominated for three more.

One of the nominations was for best casting. I was really excited about that one, because that meant us and the people we help on the show. The other nominations weren't for us, necessarily; they were for the show. Yes, the show is about the Fab Five and how we help people, but that wasn't explicitly what the awards were for. But this one felt really special.

Weirdly, an hour after we found out, we had to go shoot the show like it was just another day. It was a really jolly time on the set. That night, we had a celebration dinner with the entire cast and crew.

Then, the morning of the Emmys came. I had chosen my outfit about two weeks prior.

I had worked with a red carpet stylist for the event. There are different kinds of stylists: A wardrobe stylist (that's me) goes into real people's closets and helps them dress. An editorial or red carpet stylist is a person who has connections to designers. They work with a designer to come up with a look for a celebrity or pull looks from a bunch of designers for an editorial shoot. So in this case, I worked with a stylist whom I'd found at my *PAPER* magazine shoot.

When I'm preparing for an event, I'll tell him exactly what I want from different designers, and he'll pull the options for me, and I'll put my look together myself. Normally, with a celebrity, the stylist will pull the pieces and put the looks together for them, so they don't have to worry about it. But I am way too particular for that.

I actually don't love wearing a tuxedo. I think they're super boring. I know it can be nice to keep it classic, but looking at a red carpet, it's like, "Oh, look, another man in a black tuxedo." Do you stand out from the crowd? No. Plus, there's so much pressure associated with them—the pressure of looking your best, the pressure of keeping up. To expect a man to wear a tuxedo on a red carpet is kind of an old-fashioned request. Sometimes men go bolder, and they're criticized for it. Even a suit would be better than a tux! Why not let men be more creative with what they're wearing? I say, show your personality!

I don't love formal wear in general, because I think it embraces a very white, upper-class expectation of wealth. Since I'm not a formal-wear guy, sometimes I throw on sneakers with my tux. I don't want to look like a fifty-five-year-old white guy who goes to a golf club and wouldn't call me the nicest words behind my back. I don't love that guy, so why would I want to dress like him?

When I got my first tux for the premiere of our show, I found it only five hours before the premiere, at a Suitsupply. This was back before the show aired, and designers weren't interested in dressing a no-name. I had a stylist pull options for me to choose from, but he pulled things that I definitely didn't want, as they were either too loud or too plain. I needed to do this myself. So I went to Suitsupply and found a crème velvet jacket with a satin lapel. I knew instantly how I wanted to style it—with a white shirt, no bow tie, a skinny black trouser, and black shoes. I was in and out of the store within twenty minutes, knowing I would love my look.

I had it altered by a tailor Netflix recommended to make sure it fit me perfectly, because they knew he could turn an amazing alteration around in just a few hours.

I walked down that red carpet feeling so confident, knowing that tux highlighted my body in the very best way. I wore henna on my hands to incorporate my own culture, and I didn't wear a bow tie. No matter how many times I have to wear a tux, I'm going to find a way to make it my own.

If you find yourself in a situation where you need to wear a tux, my first piece of advice is to make sure it fits. Find a tux that works *for you* and is highlighting the best and minimizing the worst parts of your body. My next piece of advice is to find something that feels like *you*. Don't feel like you have to just wear the black tux, the black bow tie, the black shoes . . . you don't. Don't be afraid to experiment— maybe you wear a T-shirt underneath the jacket, or maybe you pair it with sneakers. Think about changing up the colours, too. A tux doesn't have to be worn in the most basic bitch way.

When it came to the Emmys, however, I knew I wanted to wear Thom Browne. I love him. His stuff is always very fitted and short, which works well on a vertically challenged person like me. He messes with proportion more than any other designer I know, and sometimes it borders on androgynous. I also love that his formal wear isn't overly formal. It doesn't feel stuffy. When I'm dressed up, I want to feel playful and young and interesting, and Thom Browne does a beautiful job with that.

The Emmys take place over a couple of different nights. We were nominated for something called the Creative Arts Emmys, which take place the week before the Primetime Emmys. These are reserved for unscripted shows like talk shows and reality-based programming. On the Primetimes is where you'll see awards for scripted shows and where the actors receive their awards.

So, because there were two nights of Emmys, we had to get two looks. The first look I chose was a simple one, because it wasn't going to be televised in such a big way.

As the big night approached, I didn't feel anxious about the awards ceremony at all. We were nominated, and that alone felt really powerful. That morning, Rob and I lounged around at the pool, got a spot of lunch, and in the late afternoon, got ready. Our car turned up at the hotel. You feel really glam walking through the lobby to get in your car, while the other hotel patrons are watching you, in awe of what you've got on. It's really exciting.

We turned up at the Emmys, where the five of us were presenting. We went backstage to rehearse with all the other presenters. It was fas-

cinating being in that space. We had been in a bubble for so long—
when we're filming the show, there aren't many times where we feel
very Hollywood-y, because it's usually just us five, in other places. Only
in situations like this do we start to think, *Whoa. We are in this.* Suddenly, you're sitting in a room with the likes of Carol Burnett and Lisa
Kudrow and Heidi Klum, and everything starts to feel really bizarre.

I was not nervous to present, and I have absolutely no idea where
that confidence came from. If you'd told me two years ago that I would
have to get up and speak in front of people, that would have freaked
my shit out. But for some reason, it didn't faze me.

As we were waiting for our category to come up, I definitely wasn't
nervous, because I didn't expect to win. To win an Emmy? I thought,
That's not my life. That's not my story. So I went into that ceremony
truly prepared not to win. There's that episode of *Friends* where Joey
is going to an awards ceremony, and Rachel tells him, "When you lose,
be graceful. Just smile and clap. Clap and smile."

Rob turned to me and asked if I was okay, and I was like, "Oh, it's
all fine." There were so many people around that I was in awe of. No
matter what happened, it was all a magical experience.

When you're nominated for an award, you don't know when your
category is going to be called. Then James Cordon was reading off our
first nomination category, for Outstanding Structured Reality Show. I
turned to Rob and said, "Oh, gosh, I'm nervous." I had to be careful
not to give too much away because the cameras were on us. Then
James said, "Oh my god, they've done it," as he looked over at us. As
soon as he said that, I was like, *Oh, shit. It's us.* And then I jumped up
and screamed, and so did my boys.

I cannot describe the feeling beyond saying that it was a complete shock. That's not me trying to be modest; it really was a shock. I took myself out of that for a moment to be like, *What's your face doing?* I knew my smile was just big and excited, and I tried to remind myself, *Some decorum, Tan. Be a classy bitch here. People are going to watch this.*

But I remember very clearly doing that thing—I don't even know what the term is—where you kind of pump your fist and chant, "Hoo hoo hoo!"

Then we got onstage, and I cried. It's weird that I cried with that, because I don't cry very often. And when I cry, I'll have tears in my eyes and they never stream down my face. But here, I broke down. I cried so hard. I don't think I understood the gravity of winning.

When you win, you go backstage and you thank the Academy on camera. I stood there and had no idea what to say. Finally, I simply said I never expected a Pakistani boy would be winning an Emmy for being on a show about being openly gay.

It felt profound, it felt overwhelming, it felt like something I never expected would be possible for somebody like me. And that was where the tears came from. This meant so much more than if we'd just won a pretty award.

We were nominated for four, and we won three. The fact that we just kept winning over and over again felt bizarre.

Even in that moment, I felt it—the profound feeling that my life changed a little bit right there. I didn't know to what extent. Maybe I still don't know. But I do know it changed, and I was so happy for it.

It still feels like a complete lie when I'm telling it.

When people ask, "Where do you put your trophy?" the answer is,

I don't have one. We don't get to take a trophy home, because we're not individually nominated as hosts.

We didn't know if we would be at the Primetime Emmys. We heard they were going to invite us, but unless you're on a Primetime show and you're nominated, that typically doesn't happen. But because we had won a few awards, and because our show is a buzzy show, a couple of days after we won, we were told we were invited to present at the Primetimes. We were told we were going to present Best Actor in a Drama, which is a very big category.

It was last minute, and it was very special that they were letting us do it. So it did feel lovely. I had an outfit booked, knowing that we were possibly going to the Primetime Emmys. I had wanted to go anyway, because I wanted to meet all these people who I was a massive fan of. Again, I wanted to wear Thom Browne, and I knew it would take very few alterations to make the suit fit right.

My suit was mostly white, with a navy and burgundy plaid. The fabric was almost bouclé, with frayed edges. The jacket hit at the high hip, with two gold buttons. The pants were slim and hit just above the ankle, and I wore them over Louboutin boots with a two-and-a-half inch Cuban heel. I felt incredible. I felt really sophisticated and weirdly powerful and strong. And I felt like the whole look I represented my personality well—it was classic, with a pop of something so much more.

The morning of, I wasn't nervous, just excited. I had seen the Emmys on TV many, many times. Weirdly, I was more excited about the Primetimes than the Creative Arts Emmys, even though it wasn't our category.

We took a limo service, and as soon as we arrived, the first person

I saw on the red carpet was Tina Fey. She is easily one of the most incredible people I've ever met. As we made our way down the carpet, we did our interviews and met a bunch of people and finally sat in the audience ready for the show to start. It was glitz and glam all the way. Even more incredibly, we were seated in the third row, which was nuts. There were the likes of Penélope Cruz and Javier Bardem right in front of us and even more amazing people all around. It felt huge.

Then it was time for us to go backstage and get ready to present. This time around, I started to feel really nervous and really anxious. We got lined up and stood in a certain position in the wings, getting ready to make our entrance. The stage was massive. I have never felt so glam in my entire life. As we waited to make our appearance, the energy took over. We started joking, "We should kiss! No one has ever done this before!" We were so giddy that the stage manager was like, "You have *got* to calm down. Get into position."

As we started to walk out, my nerves kind of stopped. We decided to hold hands, because that's what we do in our regular life. We got to the mic, and I looked out, and the crowd was full of people who blow my mind. I looked out and said, "Holy shit, Tan. You're about to speak in front of all these people."

We each had a line that was about five seconds long. Karamo spoke first, and I was going second. But as soon as Karamo started speaking, I got distracted, because Abbi and Ilana from *Broad City* started screaming, "Tan!" and making the heart signs with their hands.

So I became like that five-year-old boy in the school play who gets distracted by his mom in the audience and doesn't realize what's going on. Then I saw Claire Foy sitting in the front row. I am maybe her biggest fan. There are many wonderful actresses to come out of the UK, but when it comes to Claire, I think she's formidable.

Just then, I realized Karamo's line was ending and it was my turn.

So, I started to read my line from the teleprompter. I improvised my line a bit; I'm not sure why I thought it was okay to do that. Then comes this Beyoncé shimmy that I have never done in my life before. If you're reading this book, I want you to Google it, because it's really something that has never happened before. Then I literally winked at the audience, at the camera.

And then I was done!

I calmly watched the rest of the boys while thinking, *What the fuck was that, Tan?*

And then I proceeded to have the best day and night of my life. I have never felt as good as I did on that day.

Life has changed incredibly quickly. Because of this, I like to stay in Salt Lake City as much as possible. Back home, there are no events and no spotlights. If anything, my friends back home make fun of me for what I do for a living. They're a bunch of dicks who like to keep me grounded. We call ourselves the core crew. There are around ten of us, and we're one another's chosen family for over a decade now.

Incredibly, all the exposure hasn't changed my relationship with Rob. Every now and then, he'll get nervous, but I try to put myself in his position. How would I feel if, from time to time, he got a call from somebody *major*? He's like, "This is so fucking weird; you're Face-Timing with so-and-so like they're some person from down the street." He sees them for their accolades, while I see them for regular human stuff—the fact that they're going through a bad breakup, a hard time, a personal slump, or the fact that they don't feel like they're looking their best.

The only thing he can't wrap his head around is when the TV is on and I'll pop up in an interview. He'll say, "It's like you've produced it yourself and put it on TV!"

Until I got this job, we never had any issues with jealousy between the two of us. We're so different, and the people who are attracted to us are very different. We each get flirted with every now and then, as everybody does, but we can laugh it off.

The truth is, when people find Rob attractive, it makes me very happy. I'm like, "Yeah, that's my man! Yeah, he is hot! You should look at him! He looks great!" I've never been jealous in that way. On the whole, we have the same group of friends, but even when we hang out separately, there are no issues.

But something like fame can really shift that. Now it's no longer the guy at the grocery store who's looking me up and down but people all over the world hitting me up. In person, via email, via social media . . . Thankfully, I married an angel, and he is very secure.

For every day we've known each other, on every day we're apart, we text first thing in the morning, check in throughout the day, and call each other every night. I always start my morning text with something like, "Morning, handsome" or "Morning, beautiful," or "Morning, angel." And when I'm with him, I tell him every single day how beautiful he is. It's not cheesy, it's not corny, and it's not forced. We're very loving and affectionate with each other. And that has continued.

Rob is always assured that I find him beautiful, that he is my person, that he is the only man for me, and that I'd marry him a thousand times over if I could. The only thing that's shifted in this last year is, if anything, I remind him even more often that I'll be there forever, without a doubt. It's not that he needs the reassurance, but I think when one partner is in the spotlight, the other steps into a more vulnerable position, and I see it as my responsibility to remind him that I am going nowhere.

I thought we might struggle more with people sending inappropriate things, but thankfully, he's secure enough to know I don't care about that. We're secure together. He's watched me hold up my wedding ring when someone is clearly flirting, and he knows that I don't have time for that. I feel lucky that I have such a stable partner. If anything, I would love to trade places with him! He gets all the perks, without any of this crazy busy work.

He does find it more uncomfortable when people are overly flirtatious in public, because it's disrespectful. Now, he says he's reminded of just how many other people have come to see me as their property. Before, he was the only person who had the right to run up and give me a hug, but now it happens all the time.

I think jealousy could be a bigger issue if we weren't aware of it. Rob wanted me to do the show; he was the one who knew I could and really pushed me to do it. But he said, "Will you get so big that you'll find someone more successful and leave me?" It was upsetting to think that would ever cross his mind. It's easy to see how one partner becoming famous could create some real drama in a relationship, but luckily, Rob and I have always been so ride or die.

Despite all the changes, my life in many ways is the same as ever. When we aren't filming, my routine is just as it's always been: I go to the gym every morning, I go on a short hike or stroll, I do some laundry, I take a nap, I spend the evening with my husband. I love that I have a place that helps keep me grounded.

Whenever I'm back home, the thing I just came from feels like a dream. It legit feels like it never happened. Until, of course, I'm out and about and someone I've never met before says, "Hey, Tan!"

ACKNOWLEDGMENTS

Netflix. Thank you for being the most incredible company to work for, and for being so good to me. Jenn Levy, thanks for being a constant support and cheerleader. I know I wouldn't be in this position without you, and I'm so incredibly grateful. Bela Bajaria, Derek Wan, Brandon Riegg, and Ted Sarandos, thank you for continuing to let me work for Netflix, even though at times I don't feel worthy. And to the Netflix PR and Social Teams: you crushed it!

ITV America. The entire casting and production team. Special mention to Jordy, Gretchen, Danielle, Adam Sher, David Eilenberg, and David George. Most important, Wesley, for taking that initial chance on me that changed my life, forever. Thank you.

Scout Productions. David, Michael, and Rob, thank you for rooting so hard for me to get the show, and for continuing to champion my success.

Thank you to Caroline Donofrio for being the perfect writer and working tirelessly to make this what it is: a book I am so proud of.

Thank you to Hannah Braaten, my editor, and the team at my amazing publisher, St. Martin's Press: Nettie Finn, Laura Clark, Jessica Zimmerman, Jordan Hanley, and Jennifer Gonzalez.

WME. The entire team who have worked to make my dreams come true. Justin Ongert, Jenni Levine, Eve Attermann, Matthew Baskharoon, Francesco Sersale, Theresa Brown, and Haley Heidemann. (Thanks for the perfect book title!!)

My manager, Cameron Kadison. Thanks for keeping me sane. Thank you for pushing me to be the best version of myself, and to explore even the scariest experiences, for my betterment. Thank you to everyone at Mortar Media. Jess and Antranig, I see you.

My wonderful assistant, Jen Jones. Thank you, sweetheart. You are a rock and a superstar, and I adore you. You've made my life infinitely more manageable the last few years, and for that I am truly grateful.

Jen Lane and Rachelle Mendez. You are both formidable women who have taught me so much. I am in awe of you both.

My core crew. I fucking love you all. You are my rock and have been there through thick and thin these past ten years. Shit, we've been through a lot. Micky, Caroline, Megan, Sara, Miaken, Dana, Kimmy, Noelle, and David.

To my UK crew: Nas, Kiri, Vicky, Naz, Yas, and the whole Ali clan. Thank you for being there for me for my entire adult life. I love you.

My family. My whole immediate family and many members of my extended family (you know who you are). I don't have the words to describe what you mean to me. I am blessed to have been born into such a wonderful family.

Last but not least, my Queer Eye castmates: Antoni, Jonathan, Bobby, and Karamo. Thank you for making this the most amazing ride of my life.

Oh wait . . . and to you, the most supportive and loving fans. I appreciate you more than you'll ever know!

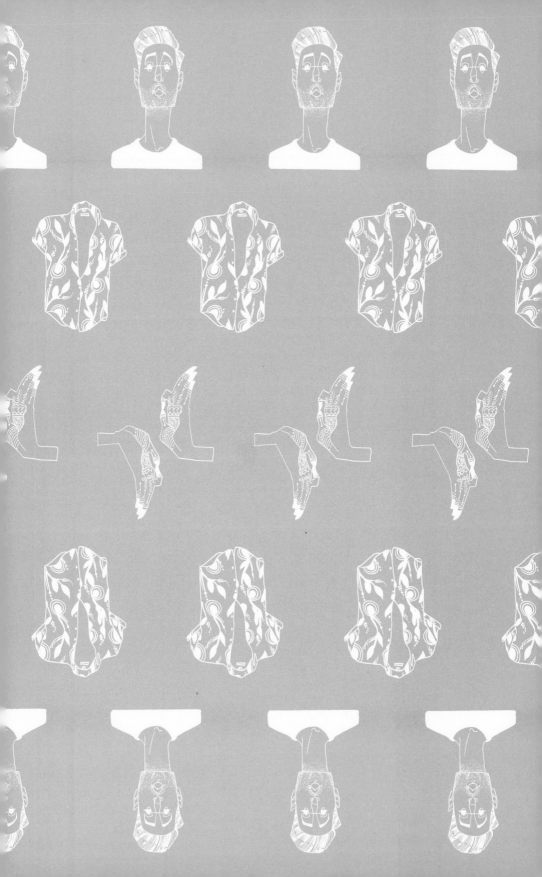